I can only hope and ... of this study, doctors ....onal fears to overanxious, ov ...autious parents and will take the time to listen to what they are saying, and truly realize that nobody knows their child better than his/her own parents.

LISA L. DIAMOND

SIDS mother who had a premonition of her infant's death

This wonderful book illuminates the premonitions experienced by parents whose infants have died suddenly and unexpectedly. Each of the authors brings a unique perspective, one being the parent of an infant who died of SIDS long before it was defined and who has brought understanding and comfort to untold thousands of other families so stricken. The others are proven investigators in the field. I find it particularly interesting and important that in their studies they have included three control groups for comparison with SIDS families. It is clear from their analyses that SIDS parents experience premonitions of doom nearly ten times more often than parents whose babies do not die. Clearly this is a signal for continued intensive study of the phenomenon. This book will bring much comfort to many parents who have not only lost their infants to SIDS but also to other unexpected disorders, and let them know they are not alone in their feelings.

HENRY KROUS, MD

Professor of Pathology & Pediatric, UCSD School of Medicine
Directory of Pathology, Children's Hospital San Diego
Director, San Diego SIDS Research Project

I think you have done a wonderful job juxtaposing cutting edge scientific research with passionate and compassionate understanding of the subjective experiences of parents of SIDS children. Your book will be an invaluable resource for medical and mental health parishioners, academic researchers, parents and relatives of SIDS children and anyone interested in the causes and consequences of SIDS.

SHELDON SOLOMON

Professor, Skidmore College, Saratoga Springs, New York

I have received with interest *The Voice Within: Premonitions of Sudden Death of Children*. Parents' vivid stories of premonitions of their infant's death as well as premonitions of relatives, friends and healthcare providers. As professionals who provide grief counseling and support to families, it is essential for us to know the factors which affect grief so we can support parents appropriately. One of these factors is experience with premonitions. In our grief program in Massachusetts, we have asked parents for a number of years to describe any premonitions they had prior to their child's death. We, too, hear parents describe their grief, guilt, helplessness and sometimes their serene feelings in response. As professionals we can listen without judgment, validate parent' experiences and support them through the grief process. This book will help us to understand the significance of this aspect of parental grief.

MARY MCCLAIN, RN, MS

Project Coordinator Massachusetts Center for SIDS
Massachusetts Infant and Child Death Bereavement Project
Boston, Massachusetts

THE
VOICE WITHIN
Premonitions of Sudden Death of Children

THE
VOICE WITHIN

Premonitions of Sudden Death of Children

RICHARD HARDOIN, MD
JUDITH A. HENSLEE, MSSW
CARRIE SHEEHAN, BA

TATE PUBLISHING *& Enterprises*

The Voice Within
Copyright © 2007 by Richard hardoin, MD, Judith A. Henslee, MSSW, Carrie Sheehan, BA. All rights reserved.

This title is also available as a Tate Out Loud product. Visit www.tatepublishing. com for more information.

No part of this publication may be reproduced, stored in a retrieval system or transmitted in any way by any means, electronic, mechanical, photocopy, recording or otherwise without the prior permission of the authors except as provided by USA copyright law.

All scripture quotations are taken from the *American Standard Version*, Thomas Nelson & Sons, 1901. Used by permission. All rights reserved..

The opinions expressed by the author are not necessarily those of Tate Publishing, LLC.

Published by Tate Publishing & Enterprises, LLC
127 E. Trade Center Terrace | Mustang, Oklahoma 73064 USA
1.888.361.9473| www.tatepublishing.com

Tate Publishing is committed to excellence in the publishing industry. The company reflects the philosophy established by the founders, based on Psalms 68:11,
"The Lord gave the word and great was the company of those who published it."

Book design copyright © 2007 by Tate Publishing, LLC. All rights reserved.
Cover design by Leah LeFlore
Interior design by Eddie Russell

Published in the United States of America

ISBN: 978-1-6024700-8-8
1. Death   2. Grief
3. Bereavement
07.06.22

This book is dedicated to the many families who have been affected by Sudden Infant Death Syndrome (SIDS) and in loving memory of their precious babies. This book would not have been possible without the courage and willingness of these families to share their experiences.

ACKNOWLEDGEMENTS

The authors wish to express their heartfelt appreciation to the parents, relatives, physicians, and friends who contributed their stories to *The Voice Within*. Their support of this project and their willingness to participate in the premonition study were critical to our understanding of the impact of these feelings on grief resolution.

TABLE OF CONTENTS

FOREWORD:
THE VOICE WITHIN

A parent's worse fear is the death of a child. Losing an infant to Sudden Infant Death Syndrome (SIDS) is particularly difficult because of the unknown nature of SIDS; it strikes suddenly without warning or reason. It robs us of the sanity of a rationale universe and replaces it with one devoid of meaning. As parents, our children are one of the most important sources of meaning for us. One hundred years from now, all we have is our children's lives and their children's lives. This book, *The Voice Within*, teaches us that there is meaning even within the horrible nightmare of Sudden Infant Death Syndrome. We learn that at times of greatest challenge for us, there is often a voice we can find within ourselves which can provide the seeds of healing for this greatest of tragedies.

The authors of this book are three of the most established and respected members of the Sudden Infant Death research community. Pediatrician Richard Hardoin is the Medical Director and a founding member of the Southwest SIDS Research Institute, one of the world's largest SIDS research centers. He was honored by President Ronald Reagan for his contributions to our understanding of SIDS. Judith Henslee, a social worker, who was likewise honored, was a member of the board of directors of the National SIDS Foundation and is the executive director of the Southwest SIDS Research Institute. She has been a co-author of numerous scientific papers on sleep physiology and its relationship to SIDS, as well as the effect of premonitions of SIDS on grieving and healing. Although she did not have a premonition, Carrie

Sheehan brings an important credential to the task of writing this book: She had a child die of Sudden Infant Death in 1955, long before there was even a name for this condition which annually in the United States takes the lives of two thousand to twenty five hundred infants. She is a founding member of SIDS Family International and a contributor to the SIDS Survival Guide, the classic text for any parent struggling to understand SIDS.

They are among the pioneers in both our scientific and spiritual understandings of SIDS. Their professional careers span the time when SIDS was misdiagnosed as pneumonia and lacked even a name, to the present time where exciting new strategies are being developed to actually prevent SIDS. They have never, however, let their scientific pursuits blind them to the human side of SIDS, the grief that every parent feels. They remember a time, not long ago, when no one would even talk to grieving parents, almost for fear the same thing would happen to them. When a terrible event occurs without reason, we strive to find reasons, all too often related to our own secret shames and fears. This can complicate the natural grieving process. In *The Voice Within*, we learn that the importance of spiritual premonitions is that they often contain the seeds of healthy grieving.

I had my first exposure to SIDS over twenty years ago, when I was first starting out as a young pediatrician in private practice. A distraught mother came rushing into my office late in the afternoon, carrying her baby in her arms. She told our receptionist that her baby was very sick and needed to see the doctor right away. My nurse immediately brought her infant into an exam room, where I was confronted with a healthy, smiling, cooing three-month-old who seemed to be in perfect health. Her bright eyes and entirely normal physical exam were in stark contrast to the sadness and fear I saw in her mother's eyes.

My professors had taught me to never ignore a parent's intuition, so I did an extensive medical work-up on the infant. I got a chest x-ray, blood work and even considered admission to the hospital overnight. Ultimately, I thought that this mother was simply having the fears that any mother could have about a baby and thought I was being cautious by having her return in the morning for another examination. The young mother looked at me with great sadness and said, "I hope my baby lives until the morning."

The next morning, I learned that the infant had passed away from SIDS overnight. I felt horribly guilty, and a failure as a physician. I found no relief in my medical texts or in reviewing the case with the physicians I trusted and respected to learn what I could have done differently. I wondered if I had what it takes to be a pediatrician, which involves the sacred trust of caring for other parents' children. Learning that even the best physicians cannot prevent or diagnose Sudden Infant Death before it occurs brought me no comfort. I was convinced that I had missed something on the infant's exam and that I was personally responsible for this mother's anguish. I attended the infant's funeral and could not even look her mother in the eye.

Several months later, I was shocked when the same mother returned to my office with an older child who presented with an ear infection. This time I looked her in the eye, and found serenity and calm there that was unexpected. I awkwardly blurted out, "What are you doing here?" I thought I would never see her again.

She said to me, "Dr. Morse, it wasn't your fault. I always knew that my baby would die. When I was carrying her, late in my pregnancy, I had a dream. I was asleep, but suddenly

I seemed to be awake. I was floating above my body, and a woman wearing all white clothes was next to me. We looked down at my body and swollen belly and she said to me in a voice I will never forget, 'You know, she will not be allowed to keep that baby.' I awoke with a horrible fear in the pit of my stomach, but soon forgot about my dream.

"The reason that I came rushing into your office that day was that I had taken a nap that afternoon. I suddenly woke up and saw the woman at the foot of my bed. She smiled lovingly at me and said, 'It's time.' I knew what she meant and rushed my baby to your office.

"You listened to me and tried to find something wrong with my baby. I have since learned that many doctors ignore or dismiss a mother's fears. Because of your thoroughness, at least I know that everything that could have been done to prevent my baby's passing was done. I will probably always cry every single day about what happened, but that lady (the lady in white) taught me that there was a reason for what happened to me. I don't know what the reason is, but it wasn't your fault and it wasn't my fault."

This was my first exposure to the lessons that we learn from reading *The Voice Within*. Every parent needs to read this book. Learning to discover our "voice within" can help to guide us not only for tragedies such as SIDS but for any of the challenges in our lives.

We learn that this guiding and healing voice can present itself in many different forms. My patient's mother had a vivid dream, which is actually one of the more uncommon forms the voice takes in communicating with us. Often parents simply have a strong unexplained feeling, something far different from the ordinary type of fear that every parent has about their children. Others will hear a voice of spiritual forewarning. Many parents will actually see something about their baby that is wrong, something tangible and yet seen only by the parent, not even to their physician. *The Voice Within* documents that these premonitions also occur to friends, relatives or even health care professionals involved in an infant's care.

"But how do we know that these feelings are real, and not some trick of the mind?" one anguished mother asked me. A physician echoed these same thoughts to me when he almost angrily said: "What right do you have to give these parents false hope and sell them a pipe dream that they had some sort of spiritual premonition? Although that sort of thing might sell books, how can a medical scientist promote these concepts? Isn't it true that everyone has these sorts of feelings, and we only remember them when tragedy strikes? And don't tell me that as long as it makes parents feel better, it doesn't matter if it's true or not. A parent struggling with the loss of a child deserves honesty from their health care professionals."

The Voice Within addresses just these concerns. We learn from reading it that science can often illuminate our spiritual feelings. The authors are first and foremost medical scientists. Their research design and results have already passed scientific scrutiny. Only after they presented this information to the scientific community, published it in a mainstream peer reviewed medical journal and presented it at dozens of scientific conferences did they take the step of presenting this information to the general public.

Furthermore, exciting advances in the past twenty years have finally resulted in a new scientific paradigm which can explain how premonitions actually work. Although far from proven, the concept that human beings have the ability to sense future events is solidly within the realm of scientific possibilities. For example, Professor Dean Radin at the University of Nevada Las Vegas has demonstrated in the laboratory that college students serving as research subjects can sense extremely unpleasant future events. He documented that they would have increases in heart rate and sweating before they were shown gory pictures, yet would not have the same changes prior to being shown pleasant pictures. A computer would randomly generate the images they were going to see so they had no way of knowing what sort of picture they would see next. Yet just like many of the parents' described in *The Voice Within*, these college students somehow anticipated an extremely upsetting future event. Often the student would not be able to describe how they subjectively felt, yet documented physical changes such as a rise in heart rate prove that on some level, they understood something bad was going to happen next.

To learn how such premonitions are scientifically possible, we turn to the dry sterile world of information systems theory. One reason I think so many of my colleagues are unaware that modern science in fact predicts the ability to sense the future is that the reading material itself is extremely dry and boring. The classic text *Living Systems* was edited by James Miller and represents the work of a large interdisciplinary team of scientists from Harvard, the University of Chicago, and the University of Michigan. Although widely acclaimed as a monumental integrative achievement of human thought, few scientists can actually get through the text. For a field with such National Inquirer sort of implications, far too often the crucial information can only be found by reading articles with titles such as "Energy Cardiology: A Dynamical Energy Systems Approach for Integrating Conventional and Alternative Medicine."

Another barrier to understanding the concepts of this exciting new science is the prejudice and superstitions of scientists themselves! Only recently have brilliant thinkers such as Gary Schwartz and Linda Russek dared to come forward with their hypotheses of how premonitions could actually work. Dr. Schwartz is a professor of Psychology, Medicine, Neurology and Psychiatry at the University of Arizona. Prior to that he was the director of the Yale Psychophysiology and Behavioral Medicine Clinic! While at Yale, in the 1980s, he developed a general systems theory predicting a universal living memory process that, of course, would be timeless. He had the most skeptical mainstream scientists he could find review his theory, and they were unable to refute it or deny its implications. Yet he never even attempted to publish it until 1998 ("Do All Dynamical Systems Have Memory? Implications of the Systemic Memory Hypothesis for Science and Society," in Pribram K (ed) *Brain and Values* 1998). In his own words, he feared his colleagues would think he had a thought disorder as "sometimes objective scientists can be as irrational and stubborn as two-year-olds when confronted with new ideas."

Since the science of understanding premonitions is a new science, far too often the important pieces are found in widely different scientific journals, which makes it hard for physicians such as my physician friend mentioned above who was so skeptical of the ethics of discussing premonitions with grieving parents. For example, recent laboratory and experimental evidence documented that the near death experiences of dying patients are real is found in a journal called *Aviation, Space and Environmental Medicine*. My own research which suggests that we are all born with an area in our brain, a "god spot," which allows us to tap into the universal memory process described by Schwartz was published in the *American Journal of Diseases in Children*. Research on past life memories was published by Professor Stevenson at the University of Virginia in the psychiatric journal *The*

Journal of Nervous and Mental Diseases. Much of the solid work on how our minds can predict future events is found in engineering journals such as *The Proceedings of the IEEE.*

Fortunately, interdisciplinary think tanks such as The National Institute of Discovery Science (NIDS) have taken on the task of integrating this diverse information and making sense of it. Brilliant generalists such as Robert Bigelow, founder of NIDS, have taken on the task of making sense of this diverse material. My interactions with the scientists at NIDS have convinced me that it is scientifically acceptable and ethical to suggest to parents that the visions they had before their infant died can be trusted and are a normal part of the grieving process.

The Voice Within is a book about love, compassion and the healing of grief. It is not a science book, although it is written in part by scientists. You will learn that we all have a voice within that we can rely on in times of great stress and need. Far too often we dismiss and ignore this inner voice. Learning how to understand and interpret this voice properly is the great lesson we can learn.

MELVIN MORSE M.D.

INTRODUCTION

"I felt he was lost—missing. I saw an empty crib—often an empty car seat. He was always gone, and I was always looking for him everywhere. I went on a quest looking for him, in dreams all over the world…as though he had been kidnapped."

The Texas based Southwest SIDS Research Institute focuses on Sudden Infant Death Syndrome (SIDS) research, education, medical care, and support for families affected by this devastating tragedy. As a national research center, the institute houses a nationwide database consisting of prenatal, birth, neonatal, and developmental histories on babies who have died of SIDS as well as control infants. As part of the research program, psychosocial factors which influence the grieving process are evaluated. One important study, entitled *The Impact of Premonitions of SIDS on Grieving and Healing,* evolved from this area of research.[1] It was first presented to a parent group at the 1992 SIDS Alliance annual conference. The response was so positive that the conference program was rearranged to allow for a repeat presentation the following day. Until the completion of this study, there was no mention in any medical or SIDS literature about families who had experienced a pre-death premonition (PDP) or acknowledgement of the further burden they carried.

The study has since been published as chapters in several books and presented to numerous professional and parent groups, including a World Health Organization meeting in Vancouver, Canada, and three international SIDS conferences held in Norway, France, and Washington, D.C. The study has also been presented at SIDS and grief conferences in Atlanta, Birmingham, Chicago, Gainesville, Palm

Springs, Pittsburg, Portland, Rochester, Salt Lake City, and San Diego.[2][3][4] Anecdotal stories have been gathered that document the occurrence of PDPs in Australia, Europe, Africa, and Asia.

While it is lamentable that at this time no intervention is known which can prevent all SIDS deaths, a review of parent narratives on PDPs indicate that acknowledgement of the reality of premonitions can have a positive impact on the grieving process. The health care professional's reaction to parental feelings of impending death strongly influences emotional healing. Anticipatory grief, when allowed to occur, may positively affect the family. Although the subjective nature of such experiences makes it seemingly impossible to judge their objective reality, it is not necessary to do so. Simply acknowledging that such premonitions are a natural and normal event can be comforting and validating to parents facing the tragedy of SIDS.

SURVIVING SIDS—AN
UNFINISHED MELODY

In 1955, very few people in Seattle could tell you exactly what a "latte" was. Probably fewer could tell you what a "Crib Death" was. Nor would anyone have known what Sudden Infant Death Syndrome was, even through it was happening in their city to two to three babies out of every 1,000 baby boomers born that year. Death certificates of infants read "acute virus pneumonia or interstitial pneumonia" whether or not an autopsy was performed. Although the sudden and unsuspected deaths of apparently healthy infants had been occurring since biblical times, the occurrence would not be named and officially recognized until the second international SIDS conference in 1969.

In the 1950s, Seattle's Capitol Hill, one of her seven original hills, became a community of young couples who would fill the large homes, the six schools, the playgrounds and nearby Volunteer Park with the baby boomers parented in the post World War II era. The incredible sense of optimism, the once again clearly defined roles for men and women, gave a feeling of well-being and certainty of a future of health and security. Under the shadow of the cross of the Jesuit parish, a center of faith for the majority of the families, security rested in God and country. In the nineteenth and early twentieth centuries almost all families had an infant's name on a headstone in the cemetery. With the use of penicillin and other medical advances, many forms of neonatal and infant death were eradicated. Families no longer expected their infants to die.

In 1954, after four years in eastern Washington where my

husband Tom had been a teacher and small town winning basketball coach, our family moved back to Seattle. I soon found myself pregnant again. Having delivered three babies in a drugged stupor, I decided to try "natural childbirth," a method which had the medical establishment embroiled in controversy. I found a doctor sympathetic to the idea of a birth with minimal medication and a husband supportive of attending the birth. At that time in Seattle, natural child-birth was so unusual that the only hospital which allowed it, Virginia Mason, was featured in *Life* magazine. The memory of the ecstasy of Molly's birth, on a summer's night in July, is still clear and would be the light that eventually helped to balance the shadow of the events which would follow.

Molly was a little strawberry blonde with a crooked smile that won everyone's heart. With a busy schedule juggling the children's summer activities, days rolled one into another. In August, we, like many other families, hosted out-of-town guests for Seattle's Seafair, an annual event that changed a rather pro-vincial Seattle into a bustling metropolis. Life was wonderful.

Not quite willing to give up the vacation feeling, we planned a "last of the season" holiday at our summer cabin on Whidbey Island. It was Columbus Day weekend and every-one planned to leave Friday after school. On that day, October 6th, Molly's godmother Betti came by with her one month old, Judith. For the infants' afternoon naps, Judith was put in the downstairs bassinet and Molly in the crib upstairs. Over coffee, we marveled at the world of the 1950s, post WWII, college behind us, days filled with children's activities, caring and loving husbands, and volunteer "white glove" activities to challenge our creative and intellectual energies.

Betti and baby Judith left. After school we prepared for our island departure. Our five-year-old went up to check on the still sleeping Molly. She came downstairs saying that the baby looked "funny." Sensing her tension, I went upstairs and though over half a century of my life has passed, that instant of discovery remains a fresh memory. Then and now, as if in slow motion, I am turning her over, my eyes bringing to consciousness tiny legs that look like white and blue marble cherub limbs, heavy as any sculpture. Nothing prepared me for the shock of her lifeless, blackened face. At that moment I lost all innocence. What was formerly a miracle of beauty and hope was silently and mysteriously destroyed.

I shouted for Tom and phoned the fire department while he attempted CPR. The children were taken away by kind friends and neighbors. The sound of the siren, echoing far off and moving closer, confirmed what part of me wanted to deny. Molly was transported with Tom in a police car to the hospital's emergency room. It was not until years later that I found out about his ordeal. He was locked in a room under police surveillance until his background was checked and suspicions allayed.

We gathered with family and friends that evening. No one actually told me that our two month and ten day old daughter was dead. I never saw Molly again. The death certificate read "acute virus pneumonia." The next day we selected a casket, and the following day Tom and I met the parish priest at the cemetery. He walked toward us with the small white casket in his arms. Tom went back to school the next day, and the following week I moderated a fashion show, which ironically benefited our children's hospital.

Do not misunderstand. Family and friends were kind and loving. The fact that the chief of staff at Children's Hospital, a life long friend of the family, called to extend sympathy, lent an authoritative sense of support. There was a small town's outpouring of love for their former coach and his wife. But none of the flowers sent or any written message mentioned death. Culturally, displays of sorrow were neither politically correct nor did it even seem an issue. Repression, coupled with words about how God had blessed us, reflected the "stiff upper lip" attitude of the day.

Such denial works for awhile. But denial, I discovered, is only postponement. My acute depression and suicidal feelings were resolved primarily through the compassion and wisdom of a dear friend who was also a psychologist and Jesuit priest. However, it was not until other losses in my life, several decades later, that I fully dealt with Molly's death.

It is difficult to believe, but in 1955 no one spoke directly about death. Certainly no one dealt directly with children's grief. Hindsight can bring deep regret but also wisdom. Tom and I had not known anyone who had shared the same experience, so there really was no way to measure whether or not our grief was normal.

What was happening on the national health scene about these mysterious deaths, later to be called "the disease of theories"? Twentieth century SIDS research in America was probably initiated with the documented studies of pathologists Jacob Werner and Irene Garrow, a husband and wife team in the medical examiner's office in Queens, New York.[5] In the forties, when exploring the relationship of mechanical suffocation to SIDS, they argued that evidence for the belief that healthy infants died of suffocation was pure folklore. Their studies showed that natural inflammatory processes were involved in most deaths.

A parents' movement began on the East Coast in 1958 by a couple, Mr. and Mrs. Jed Roe, who refused to accept their son's autopsy report of "acute bronchial pneumonia." Desiring to prevent other such deaths, and in memory of their son, they developed and funded the Mark Addison Roe Foundation. This would later become the National SIDS

Foundation, involving medical personnel, researchers, and families affected by crib death. Meanwhile, in 1961, Fred and Mary Dore's daughter Christine died suddenly and unexpectedly. At the time Fred was a Washington state legislator. In 1963, as chairman of the Appropriations Committee, he introduced a bill which mandated that autopsies be performed on all children under three years who died suddenly and their deaths studied at the University of Washington. In the fall of 1963, the university conducted the first international conference on causes of sudden infant death. As recently as 1964, the first display on unexplained death during infancy was exhibited at the American Academy of Pediatrics. SIDS was defined and its pathology described in 1969 at the second international conference. It was not until April 22, 1974, that the National SIDS Act was signed. States implementing SIDS counseling projects became eligible for research grants and federal contracts. SIDS was finally coded in the International Classification of the Causes of Death, published by the World Health Organization.[6] Today, families receive support and information from government agencies as well as non-profit groups.

Since its original definition, Sudden Infant Death Syndrome, Crib or Cot Death, has been redefined. Currently SIDS is considered to be "...the death of an infant under one year of age which remains unexplained after the performance of a post mortem investigation, including an autopsy, a complete examination of the death scene and a review of the clinical history."[7]

In the United States in the 1980s, between 6,000 and 7,000 SIDS deaths were reported annually.[8] As a result of the Back to Sleep Campaign of the 1990s, which advocates putting babies to sleep on their backs, the 1997 SIDS rate dropped to a low of 0.694 per 1,000 live births.[9] However encouraging the numbers and very recent research which identifies a potential biological cause, to families who experience the shock, trauma, and grief of their infant's sudden death, their need for empathy and compassion has not been diminished.

Dreams and Premonitions... A Historical and Psychoanalytical Point of View

The concept for a study and book on sudden death and premonitions was not to prove that premonitions exist, but simply to discover whether, if common, they were helpful and comforting during the grieving process. When our study was undertaken in 1987, few other researchers addressed this issue. By 2002, numerous books and studies focus on such phenomena, presumably because of an increasing, widespread interest in near death experiences, dreams, neurobiology, and psychic phenomena. Paving the way for such areas of study were the writings of primitive cultures, Greek philosophers and healers, and the comprehensive academic questioning of Freud, Jung and others.

The Bible records multiple occasions in which dreams or visions provided accurate information about future events. Such Biblical figures as Jacob, Solomon, Joseph, and Nebuchadnezzar experienced dreams from God which assisted them in making decisions, some of which affected whole nations.

Sigmund Freud studied the role of dreams in primitive times: "...dreams...serve a special purpose in respect of the dreamer; that, as a rule, they predicted the future...The ancients distinguished between the true and valuable dreams which were sent...as warnings, or to foretell future events, and...empty dreams...to misguide him..." Gruppe also speaks of such a classification of dreams, citing Macrobius and Artemidorus, a Greek physician living in Rome (c. 200 AD): "Dreams were divided into two classes, the first class was believed to be influenced only by the present...The second class of dreams was determinative of the future..." This included direct prophecies, foretelling of a future event, and the symbolic dream requiring interpretation.

Hippocrates, a Greek physician (460–377 BC) and traditionally accepted as the "father of medicine," believed that dreams have the capacity to reveal the onset of organic illness. Aristotle (383–322 BC) held that dreams could predict future events. Native American cultures universally used dreams to foretell the future.

In Freud's book *The Interpretation of Dreams* (3rd Edition, 1911), he states:

> I shall demonstrate that there is a psychological technique which makes it possible to interpret dreams, and that on the application of this technique every dream will reveal itself as a psychological structure, full of significance, and one which may be assigned to a specific place in the psychic activities of the waking state...

In a series of lectures that Freud gave in 1932, he voiced the opinion that what had formerly been accepted as "all the signs, miracles, prophecies and apparitions that had been reported from ancient times" had been disposed of as the offspring of unbridled imagination or of fraud in an era when man's ignorance was great and the scientific spirit had not yet reached fruition. According to Freud, these supernatural occurrences were developed to promote religion and so, while he maintained that a study did have to take place, he admitted it was within his bias of disbelief. He chose to make the study of telepathy his focus and clearly stated, "...I have committed myself to no conviction." His study of dreams prompted his interest in telepathy. While he acknowledged that it could occur in the waking state, Freud postulated that a state of sleep existed which was particularly suited for receiving telepathic messages.

In a clear and methodical manner in his *New Introductory Lectures on Psycho-Analysis and Other Works,* Freud contends that psycho-analysis may throw light on events such as thought-transference, maintaining that it is so close to telepathy that it may be regarded as the same. "It claims that mental processes in one person—ideas, emotional states, cognitive impulses—can be transferred to another person through empty space without employing the familiar means of communications by means of words and signs."

Freud collected "a whole number of prophecies concluding that not every case is equally convincing and many could have a rational explanation, …but taking them as a whole, there remains a strong balance of probability in favor of thought transference as a fact."

Dr. A.A. Brill submits the following in his translation of Freud's work:

> If we concede that we have by no means exhausted the psychology of superstition…, we must, on the other hand, at least touch upon the question…whether there are really no omens, prophetic dreams, telepathic experiences, manifestations of supernatural forces and the like. I am now far from willing to repudiate…

these phenomena, concerning which we possess so minute observations even from men of intellectual prominence, and which certainly should form a basis for further investigation. We may even hope that some of these observations will be explained by our present knowledge of the unconscious psychic processes without necessitating radical changes in our present aspect. If still other phenomena, as, for example, those maintained by the spiritualists should be proven, we should then consider the modification of our 'laws' as demanded by the new experience, without becoming confused to the relation of things of this world...

Jung introduced the idea of synchronicity:

Precognition, clairvoyance, telepathy...are phenomena which are inexplicable through chance, but become empirically intelligible through the employment of the principle of synchronicity, which suggests a kind of harmony at work in the interrelation of both psychic and physical events.

As anyone who takes a definitive stance, Jung was both attacked and applauded. The first formal presentation of his theory was given in a brief lecture—his last—at the Eranos Conference in 1951 in Ascona, Switzerland. The monograph of this work appeared in 1960. In the forward to a book he states:

As anyone can see after reading a few pages, there can be no question of a complete description and explanation of these complicated phenomena but only an attempt to broach the problem in such a way to reveal some of its manifold aspects and connections, and to open up a very obscure field which is philosophically of the greatest importance. As a psychologist and psychotherapist I have often come up against the phenomena in question and could convince myself how much these inner experiences mean to my patients. In most cases they were things people do not talk about for fear of exposing themselves to thoughtless ridicule. I was amazed to see how many people have had experiences of this kind and how carefully the secret was guarded. So my interest in this problem has a human as well as a scientific foundation.

An increasing amount of academic literature on premonitions and near-death experiences has been published in the twentieth century. Robert Jay Lifton talks about prospective dreams in his book, *The Life of Self.* In this book he provides a systematic integration of many strands of post-Freudian thought. He shows how we balance immediate and ultimate concerns—an area most psychologists surrender to the theologians.

M. D. Faber, a professor emeritus at the University of Victoria in Canada, is a psychoanalytic commentator. In his book, *Synchronicity*, published in 1999, he offers an alternative to Jung's contention that remarkable coincidences are not necessarily fortuitous or accidental and also that the world may be formally predisposed to them. Unlike Jung who invoked the supernatural or spiritual, Faber's goal is to remove the notion from the edge of the occult and ground it in wholly, realistic naturalistic terms.

Another contemporary psychologist, Dr. Joan Borysenko, had a life changing premonition in which she experienced a vivid image of her infant being burned. When the event occurred as predicted, she questioned the traditional, scientific world, wondering where the information came from and how this resource could be tapped to benefit others. She ultimately co-founded the Mind/ Body Clinic at Beth Israel/ New England Deaconess Medical Center which is affiliated with Harvard, and she has authored numerous books on the relationship between the mind and body.

Larry Dossey, M.D., experienced premonitions of future events, during dreams, which came true. These experiences caused him to question the traditional, scientific, everything is "black and white" approach to medicine. Exploring the influence of the spiritual in healing, Dr. Dossey demonstrates the powerful effect of prayers, dreams, and intuition through review of scientific studies. He brings the spiritual to mainstream medicine.

> Regardless of how we view premonitions, these visions, dreams, and feelings are very real to the parents who experience them. Their existence has an important and lasting impact on the grieving and healing process. It is the hope of the authors that those affected by premonitions will no longer fear the "thoughtless ridicule" so aptly described by Jung.

WOULD YOU BELIEVE?

In the spring of 1987, Judy Henslee, Executive Director of the Southwest SIDS Research Institute, and Carrie Sheehan, Regional Director of the National SIDS Foundation, attended the first SIDS International meeting in Lake Como, Italy. In the Villa Olna, amidst centuries old statuary and colonnades, they had a serendipitous exchange.

Judy described a call from the mother of a high risk infant followed by the Institute: "My baby is having more monitor alarms. Shouldn't we schedule a sleep study for next month? I...I..." Judy recognized the voice of Wendi, whose first infant died of SIDS two years earlier. It was clear from the sound of her voice that she was concerned about her subsequent infant. "I...something happened...it's hard to talk about. Maybe I'm going crazy. Do you have a minute?" The story that unfolded about her infant's death had forever changed Wendi's concept of reality. "I was wide awake, working in my baby's closet, when I saw her image in a small white casket at the front of our church. The vision was horrible! I dropped what I was holding and the image went away, but recurred ten minutes later. Everyone thought I was crazy. When my daughter died and we went to the funeral, my baby was placed in a small white casket identical to the one I had seen. It was the only infant casket available. I knew! If I could only have done something..."

To Judy's astonishment, Carrie shared a similar incident which had been relayed to her several months earlier when she visited Fran, a member of the SIDS support chapter in Omaha. It was the first anniversary of the death of Fran's infant son. She asked Carrie to accompany her to the cemetery on a memorial visit. The young mother then shared the feelings of foreboding she experienced during pregnancy. While watching a program about Nostradamus dealing with death predictions, she had an intense feeling of fear for her unborn child. In dreams that followed, Fran had sensations of a baby going up in the air whom she continually pulled back to earth. In her visions, this occurred in the living room of her own home. Fran's son did die in the exact location predicted in her dreams. She experienced the strong sensation of wanting to pull him back to life, but of course to no avail.

Both of the mothers were reticent to mention their experiences for fear they would be judged "crazy." Guilt, anger, and confusion reinforced thoughts that the deaths could have been prevented had they acted on the premonitions. The resultant isolation, created by an absence of any understanding of these experiences, created its own very complicated "if onlys."

Following the trip to Italy, a question, designed to determine the frequency of premonitions, was added to the Southwest SIDS Research Institute's existing database questionnaire which consisted of 274 objective questions. This premonition question was "sandwiched" between other questions, purposely worded in a benign, non-controversial way. Parents of SIDS, high risk, and control infants were asked if they "…had ever sensed that anything would happen to their baby?" Enough affirmative responses came back to justify a full study of the phenomenon. Questions to be answered by the study included: "Are premonitions normal among SIDS parents? If common, what is their impact on grieving and healing? What can be done to help these families cope with the deaths of their sons or daughters? Do parents of healthy infants also experience death premonitions which do not come true?"

By 1992, many SIDS and control families had responded to the request for information about their premonitions. Although it was a time of "information gathering," the institute had not begun data analysis. With limited funds, over-worked staff, and the never ending search for the mechanism of Sudden Infant Death Syndrome, analysis of "objective" data always seemed to be the highest priority. The study had initially become a possibility when the Board of the Southwest SIDS Research Institute gave full approval for the research. It needed, however, the full support of Dr. Richard Hardoin, the medical director and co-founder of the Institute. His strong support came. Without warning, tragedy struck the Hardoin family when Rick's mother was diagnosed with terminal cancer. As his family coped with the impending loss, the importance of "faith" and the relationship between body, mind, and spirit became increasingly clear. The depth of his deep personal loss with its anger, grief, love, and spiritual experience served as a strong catalyst for completion of the premonition study. Rick elaborates:

> Several weeks after Mom's funeral, I received a phone call from Judy Henslee, my colleague, and now the Executive Director at our Southwest SIDS Research Institute in Lake Jackson, Texas. She was bubbling with excitement about starting to analyze the premonition data! Of course if you know Judy, she is always bubbling with excitement. She could get an Eskimo excited about snow. When I heard that her partner in this project was none other than Carrie

Sheehan, the Western Regional Director of the SIDS Foundation, another boiling cauldron personality, I could only hold my breath and ask, "What is it you propose we do?" Their recollection of the premonitions discussed at Lake Como had previously gotten my attention. Gathering data seemed like such a benign thing at the time. Now, however, came the hard part. How could I, as a physician, a scientist who has prided myself in objective thinking, conduct a formal study about premonitions? This sounded like palm reading or astrology or fortune telling. Then, as I pondered the subject, I was reminded about the night of Mom's death. Dozens of questions began streaming through my head. How could that frail, semi-conscious, dying old woman muster up the energy to sit up in bed and summon her children to her side for one last good-bye? Where did that strength come from? Where did her love, her personality, and her spirit go that night when in an instant the sparkle left her eyes? And what about prayer itself? Has anyone ever seen the God we're praying to? I realized immediately that the answers to these questions and hundreds more like them are simply that there are no objective answers. Certainly there are no answers that can be scrutinized by the scientific method. You cannot measure spirit, or prayer or God like you can a blood pressure. These all come by faith alone. Yet they are every bit as important a part of life as muscles and blood. The proposed study would never be able to answer the "who," "why," "where," and "how" questions. But now I realized that didn't matter. What we could answer were the "what" questions. What did you see? What did you hear? What did you feel? What were you doing at the time of the premonition? What effect has this premonition had on your life? If enough of our parents across the country and across the world had similar experiences, I felt strongly that this study would create a cohesiveness between SIDS parents, a healing bond that could help relieve their pain and suffering. I believe this book will accomplish that goal.

From the first telling of the premonition stories, hundreds of others would follow. As the poignancy of the stories unfolded, they gained credibility and acceptance. As we analyzed the data provided by families who experienced premonitions, we began to understand how "normal" this phenomena is. Whether we are anticipating the death of an elderly parent or fearing the death of our precious child, there is an intangible "something" which transcends our physical boundaries and defies scientific explanation. Hopefully, with further information and education, medical personnel and counselors will no longer give parents reason to doubt their own reality. Through sharing of the stories relayed to us, we feel privileged to have been able to help others recognize and accept "the voice within."

THE PREMONITION STUDY

Case reports of pre-death premonitions by relatives and friends of the deceased have been reported in both the medical literature and popular press.[10] [11] [12] [13] The discussions of these experiences range from the spiritual to the psychoanalytical.[14] [15] Little is known about the incidence and nature of pre-death premonitions in control populations, so the contribution of recall bias in understanding these experiences cannot be evaluated. In spite of the strong emotional nature of these experiences, the grief and counseling literature is remarkably silent on the effects of having such premonitions.[16] [17] [18] [19] [20] [21]

Pre-death premonitions are strikingly similar to both pre-death visions and near-death experiences. An off-duty nurse reported having a premonition that a hospitalized patient she was emotionally close to had died. This involved a vivid presence of the patient "in my mind's eye," passing with the patient through a long tunnel, and finally, ending with the appearance of a bright white light which subjectively was described as "glorious, peaceful and good."[22] This event contains the core element of near-death experiences reported by survivors of profound comas and cardiac arrests.[23] Yale oncologist Diane Komp describes pre-death visions of children dying of cancer who report seeing angels, bright lights, and even Jesus driving a school bus. These pre-death visions occur to patients in the context of dreams, visions or prayer. They are described as having similarities with near-death experiences, although these patients are usually not brain dysfunctional.[24]

All these experiences are frequently described as being vividly real and superimposed over ordinary reality. They occur to patients in good mental health.[25] They can be easily distinguished from intensive care unit psychoses, transient psychotic events, schizophrenic hallucinations and drug-induced hallucinations.[26] [27] [28] [29] [30] For example, the intensive care unit psychotic event frequently involves a denial of reality, with the patient insisting, for example, that he was not near death, but actually on another floor of the hospital having a routine orthopedic procedure.[31] There are not the distortions of body image, paranoid ideation, aggressive elements, disorientation and delirium, nor illusions and delusions described in transient psychotic events.[32] One study of pre-death visions documents that the occurrence of such experiences is not related to psychoactive medications and usually occurs in patients who are not on narcotics or other hallucinogens.[33]

Pre-death premonitions have a strong spiritual component and as such would be expected to play an important part in grieving and grief counseling. Several recent review articles on SIDS do not discuss premonitions of death at all, even as a factor in counseling.[34] [35] [36] Post-death hallucinations and dreams of the deceased by family and friends have been documented;[37] [38] however, most psychiatrists and physicians have taken the position of Freud, who considered such experiences to be wish fulfilling fantasies.[39] [40] Several major texts on grieving and death and dying do not discuss either pre-death premonitions or post-death hallucinations, even though these same texts outline the theoretical importance of such experiences. For example, Rando states that issues of the perception of preventability significantly impact the length of the grieving process in SIDS deaths.[41] Premonitions of death presumably would impact the parents' perception of preventability and yet is not discussed. One important reason for this silence is that, to our knowledge, this is the first systematic case controlled study of pre-monitions of death reported in the medical literature.

METHODS

The Southwest SIDS Research Institute houses a nationwide databank consisting of comprehensive prenatal, birth, neonatal, and developmental histories on victims of Sudden Infant Death Syndrome (SIDS) and control infants. Information contained in this database was used to answer the following questions: Are premonitions a normal occurrence among SIDS parents? If common, what is their impact on grieving and healing? What, if anything, can be done to help affected families cope with their loss? Do parents of control infants also experience death premonitions which do not come true? If so, what is the outcome for these infants?

In order to better answer these questions, 174 SIDS and 164 control parents representing all 50 states and 4 Canadian provinces were initially asked in a 273-field questionnaire if they ever "sensed" that something was going to happen to their infant. Parents who answered positively were recontacted to participate in a separate study of premonitions of SIDS. Informed consent was reobtained from all study participants. Research protocol was reviewed and approved by the Institutional Review Board of Brazosport Memorial Hospital.

Participants were asked to fill out a "parental perception questionnaire" developed specifically for this study. It is a combination of "yes or no," multiple choice, and open-ended questions concerning what was sensed by the parent. For example, the first question is: "In completing an earlier questionnaire, you indicated that you 'sensed' something was going to happen to your infant. Please briefly describe exactly what you sensed." The subjects were then questioned on the timing of their experience, with whom they discussed the event, what significance they felt it had, and what they felt could be learned form the experience. Telephone or personal interviews were then conducted with these families to validate the questionnaire and expound upon their answers.

Two additional concurrent, prospective control studies were completed as a further safeguard against recall bias. 200 consecutive newborns were enrolled in a study in a suburban private practice of medicine. Parents were asked the same question at the 2 week, 2 month, 4 month, 6 month, and 12 month well baby visits: "Have you had a feeling, dream or vision that your baby will have SIDS?" If they replied "yes" they were asked to briefly describe the nature of that premonition. 197 subjects completed the full year of prospective questions.

The third control population consisted of 207 parents of every other healthy infant born in a hospital on the Texas Gulf coast. These parents were asked prospectively when their babies were 2, 4, 6, 8, 12, 16, 20, or 24 weeks of age if they ever sensed that something was going to happen to their infant. As participants in a study of normal infant sleep physiology, the Texas babies were closely followed throughout their first year of life, all medical records were obtained, and outcomes were determined within two weeks of their first birthdays.

RESULTS

In the database study group, 38 of 174 SIDS parents (21.8%) compared to only 4 of 164 control parents (2.4%) stated that they did sense that something was going to happen to their baby ($p < .000001$). 94.7% of the SIDS parents and 75% of the control parents were contacted and agreed to be interviewed. Of the two SIDS parents who were non-participants, one was lost to follow-up and one refused to participate. Interestingly, three of the SIDS parents who had written about premonitions in the original questionnaire, completed shortly after their infants' deaths, could no longer recall their premonitions. Consequently, SIDS study results were based upon responses from 33 parents, representing 34 SIDS deaths. Control study results for database participants were complied from responses of 3 parents. Follow-up with these parents revealed that 2 of the 3 children did develop problems considered to be potentially life-threatening. Review of their medical records showed polygraphic documentation of gastroesophageal reflux and apnea. Both children were treated with monitors and medication. One recovered completely after one year, and one, though four years old, continues to have documented prolonged apnea with oxygen desaturations. Five (2.5%) of the suburban control parents stated that they did sense that something was going to happen to their infant, yet their baby did not die. However, two of these five required treatment for gastroesophageal reflux and one developed chronic lung problems and continues to be followed by a pediatric pulmonologist. Six (2.9%) of the 207 Texas control parents stated on a questionnaire administered during their infant's sleep study that they sensed something was going to happen to their baby. Four of these six parents were available for verbal interviews. One of the six infants did develop significant cardiorespiratory control problems, documented by polygraphic evaluation and in-home recording. She required monitoring and use of theophylline. The mother of this infant first reported concerns about her baby's well-being prior to the baby's birth.

The majority of SIDS and control parents who had premonitions attended prenatal classes in which SIDS was not discussed. They experienced the sensation of their baby's death on more than five occasions, and reported vague, uneasy feelings without an obvious cause. The majority of these parents did mention their concern to others soon after the premonition occurred but did not visit the baby's doctor or emergency room solely on the basis of the premonition. Most affected parents reported other premonitions which also came true and stated that the premonition involving the SIDS loss occurred at least one time while they were awake.

Anxiety in control parents tended to decrease with increasing infant age. In contrast, anxiety in SIDS parents tended to increase significantly as the date of death approached. 100% of the controls in the study group, compared to only 39% of the SIDS parents, reported having had direct observation of a life-threatening event in their baby, or personal knowledge of a SIDS loss.

SIDS GROUP

Nineteen respondents stated that the pre-death sensation occurred more than five times. These were primarily vague sensations or feelings of unease. Seven had only one sensation, which was described primarily as a visual or auditory experience or dream. Seven had two to five experiences which were primarily dreams, feelings, or combinations of both.

Twenty-six respondents reported that the premonition occurred immediately preceding the death. For nine people, the experience was so compelling that they visited their doctor or emergency room. Four of these nine reported a dream or vision; two had experienced vague, uneasy feelings; and two witnessed a physical event such as apnea. Six recorded the experience in a journal prior to the SIDS death, and twenty-three told another person about the experience prior to the death. Eleven reported feeling the sensation during pregnancy, fourteen immediately after birth, and twenty-three during the newborn period.

Eleven respondents felt they witnessed a physical event, often coupled with vague or uneasy feelings. Two respondents had personal knowledge of SIDS and felt they were hypervigilant about SIDS. Seventeen described the experience as a dream or vision, and twenty-nine reported having vague, uneasy feelings without cause.

Ten reported having had previous feelings and intuitions which had not come true. Of these, two reported having dreams of SIDS which had not come true, and eight had previously had vague and uneasy feelings. Twenty-three stated that they had not previously had such feelings. Thirteen respondents reported that the experience was negative for them, creating feelings of helplessness, fear, anger and guilt. Seven reported both negative and positive feelings about the premonition, while three parents, having experienced vague fears and feelings, were left unaffected. Ten had positive feelings and felt that the experience helped them to grieve. These were primarily the same subjects with dreams and visions, although there was considerable overlap. Twenty-eight respondents stated that the experience, negative or positive, taught them to trust their own intuitions, visions or dreams.

CONTROL PATIENTS

Seven of fifteen control patients completed the parental perception questionnaire. Six of the seven reported experiencing a premonition on more than five occasions. All seven reported vague, uneasy feelings of no known cause, which occurred during infancy. However, all seven had either a personal knowledge of a SIDS loss or had seen their child apneic, blue or choking, factors which may have contributed to the parent's sense of unease. One parent became concerned after a serum alpha fetal protein level was elevated, and the feelings disappeared after a normal amniocentesis. One subject had concerns about spina bifida, coupled with uneasy feelings that the infant might die. One subject who worried that her baby might die of SIDS was at an advanced maternal age and had had two miscarriages. One patient had a vivid dream that the baby would die and had similar dreams which did not come true.

Three of the seven control infants, whose parents were available for interview, experienced serious or life-threatening events during their first year of life. Cardiorespiratory abnormalities were well documented in these babies through polygraphic evaluation and in-home recording.

INTERVIEWS

The patients seemed to fall into four distinct clinical presentations. Representative case histories of each type are presented below.

PREMONITION TYPE 1: PERVASIVE VAGUE FEARS OF SIDS

AL is a 28-year old married female from Wisconsin who has two living children. She had one miscarriage prior to a SIDS death four years ago. AL has been employed outside the home for 7 years and is in good health. During the pregnancy, she began to have vague feelings that her child would die. These continued after birth and throughout infancy up until the day the baby died. At times, she would find herself looking at her child, singing, "You are my sunshine," and then quickly think "Oh, please, don't take my sunshine away." These feelings did not accompany her other three pregnancies. After her baby's death she stated that these experiences helped her cope with the loss of her child. She thinks the death was fate, and harbors no guilt about the loss. She stated that the meaning of these experiences was "a gentle preparation and a little foreshadowing" (of what was to come). She feels she has learned not to take her children for granted and that death is a part of life.

PM, a 32-year old married woman from Texas with two living children, felt that something was wrong with her baby during the pregnancy. After the infant's birth, she went from doctor to doctor, trying to identify her baby's problem. She did not have these feelings or frequent doctor visits with her other children. She initially expressed anger at the physicians. Now PM states, "My pediatrician always listens to me now. He does not take (me) lightly. (He) thinks a mother knows what she is talking about." When asked what effect the experience had on her grieving process, PM replied, "The (feelings) helped, I was prepared for it, I knew deep down (my baby was going to die), it helped me to accept it."

Another parent with a similar experience made the comment, "In one way it (the premonition) made things better, because it helped me to get past blaming myself sooner. Yet, in another sense it made things worse, as I felt I was an over-reactor, which I am not. I don't know, it makes me crazy trying to figure it out (the meaning of my vague premonitions)."

Most other women in this category felt worse because of their fears. One mother, who took her son constantly to the doctor because she "knew" he was sick stated, "I should have made the doctor run more tests. Every parent should have their child on a monitor. I felt helpless."

PREMONITION TYPE 2: HYPNAGOGIC STATES AND DREAMS

Four respondents had vivid and unusual dreams of their child being in a casket hours or days before their child actually died. Two of them had similar dreams in the past which had not come true.

HD is a 28-year old mother of three living children who resides in Canada. She viewed her son's funeral during a dream which occurred one week before her baby's death. She stated, "(I) saw a casket being lowered. The top opened and the infant (my son) was inside." When HD went to the funeral parlor following the death, the only casket available was identical to the one in her dream. HD felt that the premonition harmed her because no one took her feelings seriously. She interpreted the experience as a warning, a mental preparation, which lessened the shock of her infant's death.

JB, a 39-year old South Carolinian with one living child, described the following dream less than one week before her son died of SIDS. She said, "He was standing up on a piece of playground equipment. I was concerned and yelled, 'Nick, you can't stand up (I thought), you're too little; you'll fall!' He heard my thoughts. He didn't speak, but I heard a little voice…in my mind. It said, 'Mamma, I'm fine.' He was guarded by two, unemotional women (angels?). I couldn't come close to him. The dream was vividly real." After his death, she had another dream, also vividly real, in which he was in a high chair, being fed by one of the same women. "I ached to hold him," she said, "but there was an invisible barrier I couldn't cross." Finally, JB reported that her own mother woke up unable to catch her breath on the night that her grandbaby died.

JB stated, "If you have a dream or vision or premonition that is 'real' compared to normal worries and speculations, pay attention to it. Maybe you could prevent a death—maybe not."

PREMONITION TYPE 3: WITNESSED PHYSICAL EVENT

Dr. K is a 39-year old physician from North Carolina who has three living children. She sensed her son "was different" during the newborn period and discussed it with her child's doctor, who could find nothing wrong. She witnessed one brief apneic event at five months of age which was not coupled with cyanosis. This occurred four days prior to his death. Dr. K was struck by what a peaceful baby her son was, sleeping a lot and rarely crying. She went into her infant's room numerous times throughout infancy feeling very anxious about SIDS. She discussed these fears with her physician, and even said out loud, several weeks before his death, "And you're not going to die of SIDS, you wonderful baby." Dr. K did not report similar fears with her other pregnancies. She feels strongly that she did not have premonitions in a supernatural sense, but, as an anesthesiologist, was making (subtle) observations about some underlying abnormality of her baby's neurological and respiratory function which led to his death. She does not feel it has impacted her grieving in any way. She feels strongly that "perhaps we should all take mothers' or caregivers' 'hunches' that something is wrong much more seriously."

PREMONITION TYPE 4: SPIRITUAL ENCOUNTER

One 26-year old Texas mother, EH, stated, "I felt that he (my son) was too good to be true. I love him so much. He was just too perfect to be mine. Looking back, I can better explain the feeling I was experiencing. I will describe it as though the Angel of Death—no…not the Angel of Death, rather an Angel from Heaven—was with us. The angel's presence felt like a patient and calm or peaceful one. It's as though the angel is in the background watching me care for (my son) until God tells him to take (my son) to Heaven. Looking back, it was a peaceful and quiet feeling of waiting." When asked what effect her premonition had on the grieving process, EH stated, "It makes me feel worse, as though I caused it by worrying."

LS, a 28-year old Ohio mother with four living children, lost her infant to SIDS at three months of age. On the night of her child's death, while LS was awake, she saw her daughter's name on a tombstone. LS heard her son say "baby cry" but thought he said "baby die." She has never had such an experience in any other context or with her other children. She feels that "the Lord" was preparing her for the death. She states that she feels no guilt and takes comfort that God is in control. She has counseled other families because of her vision.

CONTROL PREMONITIONS

JD is a 37-year old West Virginia mother who has three living children and a history of three miscarriages. During her pregnancy, she felt great fear whenever she would put her hand over her stomach. She had cold chills and continued to have an uneasy feeling throughout the pregnancy. She also had dreams which were so vivid they would wake her up. She would see her infant floating in space and crying because she could not get to her. Although her child did not die, the baby did experience an apparent life-threatening event (ALTE), with documented cardiorespiratory control abnormalities. This child continues to have severe respiratory problems at four years of age.

JD feels the experiences made her a more compassionate person. She "feels" the pain that others suffer and believes that she is a different person as a result of these premonitions.

BF, a 30-year old woman with one living child, resides in Texas. Her son, who died of SIDS, had a history of severe gastroesophageal reflux. BF sensed on many occasions that something wasn't right with her subsequent daughter. She attributed her uneasiness to her previous loss of a child. When BF also witnessed an apneic spell, she discussed her concerns with the baby's physician. She said, "I tend to get real ticked off if no one listens to me." She feels that she did the right thing in following up on her intuitions and having her child examined, especially since this child also had severe gastroesophageal reflux and significant problems with pulmonary function which did not resolve until after the first year of life.

A 32-year old married woman with one child was prospectively asked throughout the child's first year of life to record any presentiments of SIDS. This mother, who resides in the state of Washington, stated that she would be watching television and suddenly be filled with a fear that her child had died. She would often rush panic stricken into the nursery. She felt that such fears were normal and attributed them to being a new mother and feeling insecure. Even while rushing to the nursery, she felt that she was overreacting. She felt that most new mothers probably experience similar feelings and assigned no other meaning to the premonitions.

COMMENT

Study findings suggest that premonitions of death are a common occurrence among SIDS parents and an uncommon occurrence among controls. Statistically significant differences were observed, with 21.8% of 174 SIDS parents compared to 2.6% of 568 control parents "sensing" that something was going to happen to their infant. Of the 12 control infants whose parents reported a premonition and were available for interview, 50% developed significant health problems during infancy. Three of these (25%) experienced an event believed to be "life-threatening" in nature and had significant cardiorespiratory abnormalities which were well documented, two (16.7%) required treatment for gastroesophageal reflux, and one (8.3%) developed chronic pulmonary problems.

90.9% of the SIDS parents reporting pre-death premonitions stated that the premonition affected their perception of their baby's death, as well as the grieving process. These effects were observed regardless of the nature of the premonition. Premonitions fell into four distinct categories: vague impressions and feelings, dreams and hypnagognic states, physical observations, and spiritual encounters. There was no clear-cut pattern as to how any given category would affect the parent's interpretation of the premonition.

One very important aspect of pre-death premonitions is that they empower the parents who have them. Spiritual intuitions are validated when premonitions come true. This effect, which has important implications for grief counseling, was seen in the study population whether the premonition was experienced by a physician witnessing an apneic episode or a housewife having a precognitive dream.

Study participants often interpreted similar premonitions quite differently. For example, vague intuitions were sometimes interpreted as being communications from a loving God, preparing the parents for their baby's inevitable death. Conversely, some parents viewed such premonitions as a forewarning, providing them with the opportunity to prevent their child's death. Ineffective action, or failure to take any action, resulted in overwhelming feelings of guilt and anger following their baby's death. Physicians should be aware that parents who repeatedly present with their infants for evaluation of minor symptoms may be driven by premonitions of SIDS. Those parents who brought their infant to the emergency room or physician's office on the basis of their "sensations" emphasized that they did not feel listened to. The majority of parents did not feel comfortable discussing their premonition with the baby's doctor.

Exploring pre-death premonitions may result in achieving insights into an individual parent's grieving process. For example, the mother who felt that her infant's formula had something to do with her death may be at greater risk for pathological guilt than the mother who felt that her premonition meant that a loving God was caring for her child.

A review of participant narratives suggests that several interventions may be useful in helping family members cope with premonitions of death and infant loss. These include: (1) provision of a supportive environment, which encourages open discussion about feelings, concerns, and fears, (2) listening to affected family members and taking their concerns seriously, (3) performing a thorough physical evaluation on the infant, prior to the death, (4) acknowledging that premonitions are a natural and normal event, (5) validating the parent's feelings, and (6) providing on-going support, throughout the grieving process.

Many SIDS parents reported feeling that comprehensive testing could have prevented their child's death, even though they understood that there is no known way to prospectively diagnose all babies at risk for SIDS. Further research is needed on the efficacy of home monitors and the value of testing procedures for apparently asymptomatic infants of parents presenting with premonitions.

A retrospective analysis can only document a statistically significant association between premonitions of SIDS and actual deaths. However, there is also a high correlation between premonitions and the development of serious, or life-threatening events, in both prospective as well as retrospective control populations.

The vivid and intense nature of many of the premonitions in all categories makes it unlikely that recall bias accounts for the entire difference between SIDS and control groups. Only a prospective study of premonitions can validate their seemingly precognitive nature. Our intent is to fill in a gap in the medical literature and document the existence and importance of these premonitions.

THE GIFT OF PROPHECY

A Look at Strong, Unexplained Feelings

The parental perception questionnaire begins "In completing an earlier questionnaire, you indicated that you sensed something was going to happen to your infant. We want to learn more about this and how such events have affected you." Most of the responses were easily separated into the several categories that emerged. Those that were not so easily defined were simply labeled "unexplained."

In the mid 1960s an insurance business partnership was formed by Ray Mansfield and Chuck Puskar in Pittsburg. Of the two, the name of Ray Mansfield was certainly the better known. The former University of Washington Rose Bowl football alum who had moved on to the NFL Pittsburg Steelers was often noted in the press or on the screen. However, after the death of Chuck's infant son, Chuck would also become well known to many others—an honor he no doubt would have preferred to forego.

On March 24, 1976, Bryan, the infant son of Chuck and Janice, died of Sudden Infant Death Syndrome. It was a time when the momentum of the parent driven SIDS movement was accelerating across the country. Chuck explained that he became a "crusader." With the strong support of Ray Mansfield and the NFL alumni who adopted the local SIDS group as its charity, the recently identified tragedy called "SIDS" captured the headlines.

Following a meeting with other affected families in Rochester, New York, Chuck initiated a parent to parent support group. Public response was excellent, and Pittsburg formed its first affiliate chapter of the National SIDS Foundation. Chuck became active on the national scene and ultimately became a member of their Board of Trustees.

While Jan was supportive of her husband's activities and worked on resolving her grief in her own way, she was notably absent from the Pittsburg spotlight. And by his own admission, Chuck wanted it that way. He stifled her. He did not want her talking to the press because she insisted that she had had a premonition of their son's death. He felt that relating "other world" experiences would only prove counter-productive to the promotion of research and interest in this newly defined medical field. It was therefore not until eighteen years later, in filling out the study questionnaire, that Jan's premonition was publicly recognized.

In November 1975, Jan was hospitalized with placenta previa. When her condition was considered stable, she was allowed to return to the couple's high rise Gateway Towers apartment for continuing bed rest and limited activity. Two months later, on January 3rd, Jan was readmitted and delivered her son. She remembers a real "high," the delight and joyful anticipation as she looked forward to each time nine pound Bryan would be brought to her bed.

In marked contrast, however, Jan describes the experience which occurred as she prepared to leave the hospital following Bryan's birth:

> Twenty-four hours prior to leaving the hospital a feeling of edginess and anxiety came upon me. I confronted Bryan's pediatrician and my obstetrician. They attributed these feelings to my being a new mother and to the problems I had gone through during my pregnancy. I disagreed, relating that I had a lifelong gift, the

Gift of Prophesy. Although they listened with kindness, they patted and reassured me that everything would be fine. I knew it wouldn't. When I mentioned my fears at the baby's first month check-up the doctor was very kind and understanding. I told him that I had spoken to my pastor, but hadn't mentioned my feelings to my husband. I knew that I had to talk to him.

I went for my six-week check-up and again explained that I was feeling the same way I felt the night before my eighteen-year-old brother died. I was twelve years old and knew that he would die. In February, as my husband was dressing for a sports banquet held in Pittsburgh, I held the baby and said, "Chuck, please listen to me and don't think I'm crazy. Prepare yourself in some way because Bryan is going to die. I don't know when, where, or how, but treasure all your time with this precious child! Just know…I am feeling, once again, doom." My feelings continued and were especially strong and disturbing when a weekend trip for an awards ceremony took us to Florida on March 14, 1976.

Shortly after the Puskars' return, Bryan was declared dead at 9:05 AM on March 24th.

Jan maintains that having a premonition did not stop her from having a very rough five months of intense grief. With the death, however, the anxiety and edginess was immediately gone. During the road to recovery Jan realized that once again she would deal with life's difficulty and focus on learning about grief and prophecy. As reported by others in the study, Jan also had a near death experience.

She writes that she feels experiences are a God-given gift that occurred to her at a young age "for the heartbreaks that life bestows and also the good it bestows." She wrote that after the eighteen years since her son's death, her activity as a parent contact with SIDS families has opened doors for them. They realized that finally someone understood them, that they could speak and share their experiences without someone labeling them as crazy.

Amy had twin daughters but treated one infant, Cory, differently. Amy explained that she felt death was near her family and remembered that death had not "hit" in ten years. At times she would "fly" Cory around the house saying, "Fly like an angel," but when she tried it with the other twin Dara, it just did not feel right. On the night before Cory died Amy sat down and sang "Silent Night" to Cory and started crying while telling her how much she loved her. Her husband later confessed he also had premonitions, but both parents thought that these were warnings that they would have to be especially careful when the twins started walking. Interestingly, Amy wrote on her questionnaire, "Cory also felt much older than she was."

After the death of their infant, Amy and her husband have felt her presence, once vibrating and filling the space of the room. Sometimes feeling guilty, Amy knowing that Cory was going to die, regrets that she "couldn't put the clues together." She regards the experience as a lesson in trusting the gut instincts that you have.

Dr. L was an intensive care resident during her pregnancy with baby M. "Doctors are paranoid by nature of their profession about their children's health," Dr. L recorded. She sensed something devastating was going to happen to her older son and thought it had to do with his kidney problem. A workup was to be done but had been delayed. Dr. L said that she had a feeling of impending doom. Both she and her husband's lives were stressed, and Dr. L remembers praying to God not to have any of her sins taken out on the children. She also asked the Lord for guidance, questioning if there was anything she should be doing differently.

Four to eight weeks before term Dr. L had heightened anxiety. Immediately after M's delivery, however, she reported a lessening of the uneasiness. Two weeks before M's death, while thinking about the Kenny Loggins song "House on Pool Corner," Dr. L contemplated that "The Rainbow Connection" would be an appropriate song for a child's funeral. She then felt bad that she had that thought while in her oldest son's room.

Dr. L switched to an "on call" assignment the day before M's SIDS death. She had wanted her husband (who was usually more involved with his sons than his newborn) to feel the closeness to the infant that she did. To Dr. L's delight, her husband called her at the hospital to say that they had "connected."

A very sensitive doctor friend, Jacque, with whom Dr. L had not spoken for about six months called with a feeling that something was up. Since Jacque was a urologist, Dr. L assumed his concern related to their older son and promised to schedule the long overdue "workup." The next day Dr. L had strong feelings that she should not take M to daycare, but realized she would be too tired to care for her infant after being on call all night. Later that day a call came from the daycare that M, who was in a stroller, had become comatose. An ambulance had been called, and because a pulse was found, the infant was put on life support that Friday. It was withdrawn the following Tuesday.

Driving home after M's death and crying at a stop light, Dr. L saw two white doves on a traffic island in the middle of the freeway. It left her with a "powerful" feeling. In her return home she went into her bathroom and remembered strongly an experience when she had taken a bath with M, who was frightened at first in her placement in the large tub, but then relaxed with enjoyment. Dr. L called to her husband to share this. The memory came back when she saw the shower curtain and she had a feeling of joy, sensing that M was saying, "Hey Mom, it was good." That night Dr. L was awakened about 2:00 AM, and in a hypnogogic state she saw a bright light, in a field of darkness and saw a little girl with two baby figures floating to the bright light. She has had other dreams about M since her death that have been a help to her in her grief.

She feels the experience of her daughter's death has been a positive one even though it was a torment. She states "It was meant to be" preparing her though nothing could be done. She hopes it means something beyond what we see. As a doctor, she cannot believe that babies can die of SIDS—that it cannot be prevented.

Noteworthy, among many of the mothers whose premonitions were listed as unexplained feelings, was an observation of their infants' special look or stare. Angie wrote, "The day he died I had an eerie feeling about my baby as he held my finger. I said to myself, 'he doesn't want me to go to work today.' He had such wise eyes that day and was very quiet and withdrawn." Likewise, Mariane's infant, Tyler, gave her a very serious "adult" look on the morning of his death, "Very unlike his regular baby look." Ryan had a special "stare" according to his mother, Geraldine. His last look was a strong communication with his eyes as he was looking at her over her husband's shoulder. Lisa sensed that her infant Wayne seemed different from "moment one." That he was a peaceful, quiet baby did not concern her. Lisa wrote,

> He seemed to look around a lot and open his eyes staring at me. It was a penetrating type of feeling. I also told people that it looked like he had the weight of the world on his shoulders. I directly sensed that he wanted to tell me something that he couldn't express it. I felt that it was bonding with him. When he died, I immediately wondered if he was trying to prepare me for this event.

Each of these mothers had older children. Their SIDS infants were not their firstborn.

Feelings of uneasiness and apprehension about a future event affecting their children are not limited to parents of infants. The following is an example of a father of a young woman, who literally became sick with anxiety prior to her sudden, unexpected death. Although he was not able to verbalize a focus for his foreboding, the intense dread left as the death occurred.

On March 29, 2001, those on the West Coast that were watching the late night news saw dramatic pictures of a Gulfstream jet from Los Angeles that had crashed at 7:01 PM in Aspen, Colorado. Snow swirled around the mountain scene in which all eighteen aboard were killed. They were a group of young men and women, many of whom had been friends since grade school. A common denominator was their parents' involvement in filmmaking. The trip was a birthday celebration gift for their children.

Earlier that day in Hawaii, on the island of Maui, Joe Smith and his wife were getting ready to return to Seattle from a vacation that had begun on March 15th. While the anticipation of the vacation had been most pleasant, Joe had an unexplainable sense of discomfort about the flight the day before leaving for Hawaii. As a former military officer and businessman who had done much flying, the sensation was a very rare and ominous one. Despite an uneventful flight to the islands, an uncomfortable gnawing feeling was present and intensifying during the entire vacation. It was worsened by nightly dreams of planes crashing. The unnerving sense of sickness invaded his very being, rendering the trip frustrating and ruining his vacation.

On March 29th when it was time for the couple to fly back to Seattle, Joe had to deal with irrational worries about flying home and "would have taken a boat" were such transportation available. With trepidation but strength of will he boarded their plane. Inexplicably the feelings of dread and paranoia left three hours into the five hour flight. The time coincided with that of the Colorado plane crash.

After a late night arrival at his home, Joe remembers checking the mail, with the TV on in the background. An announcer said it was not known if any movie stars were aboard a recent plane crash. It prompted Joe's thought, *So you have to be a star to make the news.*

The next morning, after a dreamless night, Joe arose at 6:30 AM. As he drank coffee and glanced at the newspaper, he noticed a snippet on the front page about the plane crash. He reflected briefly on the tragedy but felt a total disconnect from it. Shortly after Joe arrived at his place of business he received a call from his ex-wife, their daughter's mother. She told him the tragic news that their daughter Lizzy was among the Aspen victims. She had been on the flight with her fiancée, and they had planned to announce their engagement and purchase the wedding ring while on their trip.

Joe confronts his trauma and grief by speaking openly about it. He has not been able to focus on his "vacation" experience and admits he cannot understand the basis for his overwhelming sense of foreboding.

On Joe's birthday, shortly after his daughter's death, he felt her presence and heard her say "Happy Birthday, Daddy." In his book *Parting Visions,* Melvin Morse mentions that death-related visions are a common paranormal event occurring in more than ten percent of the population. In spite of this knowledge, many grief counselors and psychologists consider these to be hallucinations and some go so far as to say that their visions mean nothing. To the parent experiencing such death-related visions, they mean everything. Frequently such visions of a dead child offer peace to the parent, reassuring them that the child is comfortable and safe. They treasure such moments, however fleeting, when they can feel their child's presence.

Leaving his child in daycare, Russell felt that he would never see his baby alive again. Crying all the way to work, Russell indicated that he had never experienced such strong feelings of impending loss. Sadly, his feelings proved valid.

Kimberly, a SIDS mother, reported similar feelings. Prior to leaving home she was overwhelmed with the feeling that her baby would die in daycare. Kimberly mentioned to her husband when preparing to go to work that she was "having a very hard time leaving." As with Russell, Kimberly's premonition came true.

Several families whose infants died in daycare experienced guilt at not being with their infant at the time of death. However, many felt that their strong feelings resulted from the tremendous bond they had with their babies and offered hope for the future. This common theme was expressed by one mother: "I always felt that my daughter's spirit was so strong and it's eternal. When I think back to these experiences it's comforting because it makes me feel that we will be together again some day."

"He Was the Baby in My Dream..."

A Look at Hypnagogic States and Dreams

Those premonitions in the category defined "dreams" were easily identified and also included premonitions experienced by those in a hypnagogic state (that state between sleeping and waking).

Julie recalls:

> I was involved as a subject in a psychology graduate study using hypnotherapy when I was twenty-one years old. I had a vision of a baby sitting up playing with something in its lap. I could only see the baby's back. The professor asked me to walk around the baby. As I did, I saw the baby was playing with a gun and that the baby looked just like me. Suddenly the infant was sucked down a chute, landing on an operating table in a dark, underground, cellar-like room with one bright light above. Emergency room doctors and nurses swarmed the table attempting to save the child. But I knew the baby was already dead. When I was awakened from my trance, the entire nightmare was etched in my memory. Ten years later I was pregnant with my first child. I worried for months about the "dream." But when they handed Hannah to me for the first time with

my eyes closed in fear, I slowly opened them and could see she was not the same baby I had seen under hypnosis. A huge rock seemed to be lifted off my shoulders. I never worried about Hannah again. Seventeen months later my son Noah was born and when the doctor handed him to me, he looked just like me. He was the baby in the dream.

Noah died three months later of Sudden Infant Death Syndrome.

Julie's dream was tape recorded by a Michigan State University graduate student. Although Noah's death was anticipated, Julie was uncertain on her questionnaire about the effect her dream had on the grief process. Interviewing Julie more recently, she now believes there is an "energy" out there that perhaps, someday, we will be able to tap into.

Chris experienced a dream during her last month of pregnancy which forewarned of a loss.

During my last month of pregnancy, I dreamt of a white casket. It disturbed me so much that my husband and I talked about it. I was really upset because I thought that it was my own, not ever thinking that it would be for one of our children. While I was still in the hospital, it was probably the day after Chandler was born, I remember sitting up in bed and looking at the bathroom light and hearing a voice come over the right side of me saying that I was not going to see him grow-up. I had a feeling that would come and go. Like "You better hold him now because you don't know what's going to happen or if you'll hold him again."

On Friday, three days before her infant's death, Chris discussed her fears with both her husband and the infant's doctor.

Chandler died on a Monday evening…just three days after we were at his doctor's office for a check-up and shots. I mentioned my concerns then…I remember saying exactly, "I fear this baby is going to die of SIDS." My doctor's and my husband's jaws just dropped. But my doctor reassured me that everything was fine and he was healthy…Chandler died on a Monday evening…It was that morning that I was holding him, stroking his head, and it wasn't anything said but it was like my spirit was acknowledging that I wasn't going to see him grow up…I remember…looking into his eyes and saying to myself inside "I'm not going to see you grow up, am I?" His little eyes beamed back at mine. It was something that I couldn't explain. But there was always something in his eyes, and I miss those eyes very much…!

Chris experienced another dream the night Chandler died: "…I remember having a dream that he came back one more time to say goodbye. We got to hold him, and both my husband and I were holding him up and playing with him. I remember saying in my dream, 'We must be dreaming...We must be dreaming....'"

Lynn, who lost her daughter to SIDS, had experienced dreams forewarning of death in the past. She explains:

> I have had many dreams and nightmares in my life, but I always know the "premonition" dreams because I wake up with a sick feeling in my stomach and I can't get my mind off the dream for weeks. Soon after I finally get my mind off them the "something" will happen. I had such dreams one month prior to the deaths of my two brothers in car accidents. Then I didn't have any for a couple of years—until my daughter was born. I was in the hospital the day after having her, and I was still exhausted. Everyone finally left so I could get some sleep. I had received a pink lamb musical wind-up planter with a large helium hospital balloon attached. As I slept I dreamed that the lamb broke...I could see my baby with the balloon tied around her neck floating up to Heaven. The baby looked grotesque, and I was horrified. I knew, however, that it wasn't my daughter Mandy, but that it was my child. I woke up very upset. The nurses came in to calm me. I told them I had had a bad dream, but wouldn't describe it to them. I don't know why except that it felt too real to me. They gave me a sleeping pill. I awoke the next day when my husband came in. I told him about

the dream. He didn't say much. Over the next days and weeks it was so busy it was forgotten. My next "feeling" came one and a half years later when I was in the doctor's office and found out I was pregnant again. I was happy, and we were talking. Then she told me the due date was April 28th. That date struck that sour feeling in my stomach. It was my mother's birthday, but she had died thirteen years earlier, and the overwhelming feeling which came to me was that this child was going to go and be with her. I love my mother and told myself not to be silly. I suppressed the feeling. A few days later I told my dad about the due date. It struck him as funny also. My dad, too, has had a couple of "dreams" in his life. We are very much alike. We didn't speak of it any further. The rest of the pregnancy went without incident. I was happy, but subdued. I always had a vague feeling in the back of my mind which I carefully ignored. After the baby was born everything was fine the first week or two. Only there wasn't the help that was available for my first one. My husband was working a lot more, my helpful stepmother was busy, and my dad was back to work. This baby was much harder than my first, plus I had two young children now. I quickly became very sleep deprived and depressed. After about two weeks of being home…and up until about one week before my baby died, things didn't go well. Roy would come home tired, and the baby would be crying of colic. Mandy was feeling ignored and was acting up, and I was exhausted and very hard to get along with. I was nice to the baby even though he was driving me nuts. I continued to feel vaguely that something was wrong, especially when he cried. I would hear this very high-pitched desperate quality. Other people heard it too. You just couldn't feel you did enough for him. He only smiled once a day when Roy came home from work and Markie would hear his dad's voice. I dismissed these feelings to my exhaustion. Then when he was two and a half months old, Roy had a day off… He gave me some time to myself and watched the kids while I went out. When I came home, he indicated that he had had a nice morning. Things were starting to seem better. After I had been home a few minutes I noticed that the pink lamb planter with the music wind-up had gotten broken while I was gone. I blew up when I saw it and started screaming at Roy. He got angry at my reaction initially, then just calmed me down and said "What's the big deal, we broke it having fun. We need more fun around here." Of course I realized I was being silly. I apologized and told him I just freaked out because it reminded me of that dream. Soon forgotten, the next week was wonderful. Markie was starting to sleep more, no more colic attacks from 5 to 8 PM every night, no bleeding diaper rashes. Mandy and I were finally having a little time together. A wonderful week…until the end when I found him dead with no warning. I had only checked him from a distance the previous one and a half hours. When I picked him up he looked grotesque—just like in the dream from what seemed so long ago, pale, sick-white, hard with rigor mortis.

My "dreams" are infrequent, but they are real. As much as they bother me they are also a comfort. I know there is something beyond, and I feel it is warning me…to help me cope. I do know that feeling his presence those few precious hours after he died helped…

Gina, whose husband was an emergency room physician at the time of their son's death, observed congestion in her baby. She had several doctor appointments for her son in hopes that the situation could be identified and corrected. She was assured of the infant's good health. But her concern grew as a dream compounded her fears so strongly that she immediately made arrangements for her son's baptism because she sensed that he would not be with them long. He died as plans were being made for the christening party.

Gina described her dream:

About a week before my son died, I dreamed of being in the middle of a Civil War zone. Gun and cannon fire and explosions were taking place around me…My son and I were hiding behind some barricades. Suddenly someone began shooting toward us, so I decided to pick up my son, in order to protect him. As I held him over my left shoulder to run away, two bullets hit him in his back. He died with a startled expression on his face.

She felt that her experiences were warnings and that one should trust one's instincts. She concluded, "I feel that I should have listened to my heart, even though the doctor told us that my son was fine and normal."

Nancy Maruyama is currently a grief bereavement education and training coordinator in Chicago. She has given many presentations at national and international SIDS conferences, the American College of Emergency Physicians, and hospital Grand Rounds. In addition, she has published on the subject in the Journal of Emergency Medicine. This specialty, which in a sense chose her, had not been a part of her future plans in nursing.

Nancy worked as a registered nurse for six years to help pay her husband Rod's social work graduate school expenses. Following his graduation in 1984, they made plans for the first child they so desperately wanted. Pregnancy soon followed. After a prolonged labor, eight pound nine ounce "beautiful, happy, smiley" Brendan was born on June 1, 1985.

When Brendan was three months of age, Nancy began having vague, uneasy feelings without any obvious cause. She mentioned her concerns to her pediatrician. Like so many others, she was told that Brendan was a healthy, big boy, with normal growth and development, a normal delivery, and good Apgar scores. And there was "nothing to worry about."

Nancy took the maximum maternity leave before returning to her nursing career. One day, after she had been back to work for about five weeks, she took Brendan to the babysitter and remembers the wistful look, as if he "couldn't look hard enough. He was memorizing my face." She had awakened in a cold sweat from a dream at 3 AM that morning. In the dream she was chasing her mother and sister-in-law who had her son wrapped in a plastic dry cleaning bag. She was screaming for them to give her back her son, to give her back her baby. "My mom told me it would be hard, but I would 'survive' and to have faith. I fell to the ground exhausted." On that day, October 18, 1985, Brendan, who was a healthy nineteen and a half pound infant with five teeth, died of SIDS at four months and eighteen days of age.

The day of the burial Nancy dreamt that she was walking in the alley behind her house when she saw a couple carrying her son. She elaborated,

> I asked them how they got (this) baby. They said the parents couldn't be there, so they were taking care of him. They let me hold him. Through eye contact it was without a doubt my son and he communicated to me that he was safe, happy, and okay. When I finished talking to Brendan, he smiled at me. I gave him back to the couple, and we all went on our separate ways.

Nancy has pulled strength from that dream many times. While initially guilty and angry with herself because she could not "fix everything," Nancy says she never was angry with God. Instead she relied on her appreciation of her husband's Buddhist faith as well as her own Catholic faith. By sharing her experiences, she feels newly bereaved parents often learn and are comforted.

Lisa also experienced vague, uneasy feelings prior to Brian's death. She stated that everything seemed "too good to be true" during the pregnancy and early infancy.

I had a deep feeling that something might happen to Brian. I especially feared him getting a cold. These were pretty vague feelings. Then, three days before Brian died, I had a dream that he would die on the bed at the babysitter's house—exactly where he did die. It was very vivid. It was light with sunshine, and I could even see the print on the sheets. I felt that he would suffocate for some reason, even though I didn't see any pillows around him. Brian died during his late morning nap.

Lisa felt guilty at times for not taking the premonitions more seriously. She was uncertain whether it was a warning or something to get her prepared.

These questions go through my mind often. I really am unsure. Maybe God gives us these premonitions to help us accept it easier. Or, maybe God was trying to tell me that something was wrong and he wanted me to do something to change it. I hope that parents would take their instincts and premonitions more seriously...

Janice also had a vivid dream prior to her son's death.

I had a dream that I would awaken and find my son dead in his bed. I told my husband about it, and he said it was because I had attended a funeral that day. But it wasn't. I've had a lot of dreams that have come true. This dream felt like those...

Five days later I woke up, went in to check on my son, and found him dead. Everything was exactly as I had seen it in my dream.

Although Janice said that she felt "eerie" about her ability to tell the future, she interpreted the dream as God's way of cushioning the effects of death. She has experienced dreams which forewarn of "bad things to come" since she was a teenager.

Another mother described a dream in which her precious baby died and was placed in a white casket with pink ribbons. She was so certain that her dream would come true that she discussed the need for funeral planning with her husband, focusing on the need to pick out a casket and burial clothes. Shortly thereafter, at just over one month of age, the baby died suddenly. The diagnosis was SIDS. The infant died exactly as foretold in the dream and was buried in the same casket. The mother felt that the infant was a gift from God. When the infant was alive she felt that her life was "too good to be true."

Carla was the mother of a six-year-old son and a three-year-old daughter when Jacob was born in 1990. He had been a happy, peaceful infant before his death at seven months. However, the night before he died his fussiness and crying had been very unusual. After a session of holding and walking with him, Jacob settled down and Carla went to bed. She dreamt that he had died. When she awoke and went to Jacob's crib, she found him dead exactly as it was in her dream.

The experience was so haunting for her that she "kept running away from the dream," told no one, and could not deal with the reality of her experience. She felt she had done everything "by the book." Jacob was sleeping on his back, but she now feels that if she had taken Jacob to the doctor prior to his death, he would be alive today. Following the death she had dreams in which she tried desperately to keep the infant awake, not letting him sleep. These dreams have subsided, occurring only once in awhile.

Two years ago Carla had an infant daughter. She admits she has difficulty with a burden of concern. Her teenage children tease her about her anxiety with the new baby, and she realizes it is done in an effort to support her in alleviating some of the anxiety. Carla has been unable to think of any special meaning that her experience has had and admits that she is not comfortable sharing these feelings in a group.

A staff member of the Southwest SIDS Research Institute experienced a "vision" while in a hypnagogic state. Shaken by the image of a small casket at the front of a church, her first impulse was to fear for a grandson who had significant health problems. Just three days later she found herself attending the funeral of a friend's premature infant—in the same church and in the same casket seen in the vision.

PARENTAL OBSERVATIONS

"The Doctor Wouldn't Believe Me"

One group of SIDS mothers and fathers believe that their premonitions were based upon the physical observation of an abnormal symptom. Typically, these parents reached out for help prior to the death, but their worries were discounted by their physicians or significant others. Their touching stories follow:

"He had trouble breathing and was congested since day one. He cried around the clock, and sometimes he seemed like he was in severe pain. We did let the doctor know all this, but he said that he was just an unhappy baby."

The night before their baby Michael died, Ginny and her husband took their baby to a local emergency room. Again they were reassured that he was fine. Prior to leaving the emergency room, Ginny's husband told her that he would press for hospital admission if she didn't feel comfortable with the physician's assessment. Ginny, with some misgivings, decided to take her baby home.

Ginny continued to feel nervous and uneasy, with heightened concern for her infant. As she walked toward the baby's bedroom with the sleeping infant over her shoulder, she saw their reflections in a mirror. According to Ginny, she knew, at that moment in time, that her child would die that night.

Frustrated by her attempts to obtain medical care for her son, she felt powerless to avert the impending tragedy. Unable to sleep, she cleaned the house until 3:00 AM so that it would be clean for the family members she knew would attend her baby's funeral. Arousing from a fitful sleep early the next morning, Ginny found her son dead, a victim of Sudden Infant Death Syndrome. The pathologist's report confirmed his healthy appearance:

> This 3 ½ month old boy was found dead in his crib...He had no significant prior illness and had been a healthy baby...(He)...had a minor upper respiratory infection for a week. He was a healthy infant from birth except for a few episodes of colic. On the early morning of August 26th, the parents found him dead in his crib. Clinical and pathological diagnosis: Sudden Infant death Syndrome.

Ginny stated that "sensing" that something was going to happen to her baby did not make grieving easier. She blamed herself because she didn't trust her instincts enough to seek another medical opinion. She concludes: "A mother should push her truth as hard as she can, even though she might be wrong at times. At least she will know that she has done everything within her power for her child..."

Traci also observed worrisome symptoms in her infant. She stated,

> Every once in a while Kyle would make a gagging sound, and it always scared me. I would pat him on the back. It never happened while eating so I never knew what it was. A couple of times he was sleeping and I picked him up and patted his

back. One time it happened in the car while he was in the car seat. I was frantically trying to get off the highway and by the time I did, he was okay. My husband felt he could get himself out of it without assistance. My pediatrician said it was normal. When Kyle was six weeks old I took him to the doctor because he cried and screamed so much. I was afraid something was wrong. When I got to the office I cried with the baby. That's when they said it was colic...

Traci had a difficult time coping with Kyle's death. She explains "I am having an *extremely* difficult time with my guilt of not doing *something*. Mainly, I feel I let him down as a mother and protector."

Sherie also felt concerned about her daughter.

After my baby was born and they placed her in my arms, I felt as if she wasn't mine or she wasn't meant to be with me. Two days after birth, my husband and I attended a Baptismal preparation meeting at church. The Deacon mentioned infants dying before Baptism and this weighed heavily on my mind...The few weeks she lived (seven weeks), I noticed her trembling when she cried...I called the pediatrician twice about crying and trembling...first when she was ten days old and the second time when she was five weeks old. The night she died, she was bundled in white, and I envisioned her as an "angel."

· · · · ·

Anne described her son's unusual behavior following polio, Hib and DPT shots.

> That night he failed to sleep at all. Not crying—just very "wired" as if on drugs. I rocked him all night. Tuesday through Thursday he wasn't eating as much as he had been and had a stuffy nose that a humidifier wasn't able to help. I was breastfeeding and actually had too much milk—which was *not* normal as he was always a big baby (ten pounds, five ounces at birth) and a big eater (fourteen pounds at death, nine weeks later). I called the doctor's office Thursday afternoon, but he was out and the nurse said if the baby wasn't crying I shouldn't worry…I wanted to take the baby to the doctor, but since he wasn't available at the time, I was told to come in the next day if I was still worried. The next afternoon he died during his afternoon nap. The babysitter said he fussed a little that morning, which wasn't normal for him, and didn't drink his bottle.

When asked what affect her "sensing" that something was very wrong had on the grieving process, Anne explained: "At first, I blamed myself for not taking him to another doctor. Then I was angry at the nurse who told me not to worry and at the doctor who immunized him prior to his death." Anne concludes:

Please continue serious research by asking us questions or by letting us tell you what we saw. We have natural instincts which are part of the natural cycle. Use us, the parents, as valuable research sources. Don't shut us out for fear of "hurting" us or "bringing up old memories." We miss our children and nothing will change that. We are survivors and none of your questions can hurt us anymore than we've already been hurt by the death of our children. We want to help. We owe that to our children—ourselves.

"I HEARD A VOICE,
LIKE MY OWN..."

Spiritual Forewarnings

The salt grass blew lazily in the hot Texas breeze. Sea gulls swooped to catch darting silver torpedoes swimming in schools in the Gulf. Operas were sung, plays and symphonies were performed, and museums were visited. Astronauts trained, amusement parks flourished, and malls were swarming with the daily droves of shoppers looking for a good buy. Oil wells pumped, cattle grazed, and horses rodeoed. The Gulf War seemed far, far away from the daily hustle and bustle of the ever-growing city of Houston; a city renown for its world class medical facilities, a city in which medical miracles could truly be expected to happen.

But for the infant son of one young doctor, newly graduated and with a busy family practice, medical miracles were not to be. And this unalterable fact, the impotence of Dr. R to stop the death of his precious son, shook the very roots of his reality. A physician who had studied tirelessly to achieve his dream, Dr. R described his experience:

> During the first trimester of the pregnancy I sensed that the happiness his birth would bring would not be long lasting. A few months before birth, I would, on occasions, find myself contemplating a nearby cemetery, now where my son is buried. The day he was born and I first held him in my arms, I felt, for no apparent

reason, he, my son, was not supposed to be with us. Probably two to three weeks before his death, I would be awakened from my sleep and think about SIDS. The day before he died, a voice sounding very similar to my own, would repeatedly say, "Take a good look. This is the last time you will see him."

According to Dr. R, his fears intensified when his wife planned to visit her parents and take the baby with her. They lived in another state and a flight was required. Despite his strong feelings of impending loss, Dr. R did not share his fears with his wife. However, he argued that the baby should remain at home. His wife, lacking any knowledge of her husband's concerns, insisted that her parents see the new baby. Although he desperately wanted his son to stay, he finally agreed to the trip. When he took his family to the airport, Dr. R was flooded with negative feelings. As they walked to security, he heard a clear voice warn him that he would never see his son again. As he walked to the parking lot, the voice kept telling him to go back, to get his infant. When Dr. R reached his car, the voice got softer, and then stopped. His wife called early the next morning and was hysterical, saying that their baby was dead.

When asked what effect, if any, the premonition had on the grieving process, Dr. R replied:

The process has not been a shock to me since I knew before hand that this was going to happen. The only thing I didn't know was when and where…I have no idea of its meaning. The only thing I can say is that perhaps if I would have listened to "my heart" many mishaps could have been prevented…I think people have the ability to perceive things and give it a purposeful meaning which can be used for any future event.

So strong was the impact of this experience on his life that Dr. R stopped practicing medicine for a year following the death. When he finally did share the premonition with his family, an aunt stated that she also "sensed" that something was going to happen to this baby, but was reluctant to relay her feelings.

Another family saw a "spirit" or apparition on two occasions prior to their baby's death.

The day before Ryan died, Donald (my husband) saw a tall, thin shadow at the baby's door. He did not tell me about this. The day Ryan died, I also saw a tall, thin shadow against a window. We were startled when we shared these experiences, not frightened. Ryan had a strong ability to communicate with his eyes. As he looked over his father's shoulder at me, I sensed that this stare was a final, or last look. These experiences have strengthened our faith in an afterlife and in God…

Spirit is defined as

The principle of life and energy in man and animals, at one time regarded as being composed of an especially refined substance, such as breath or warm air, separable from the body, mysterious in nature, and ascribable to a divine origin... An entity conceived of as that part of a human being that is incorporeal and invisible and is characterized by intelligence, personality, self-consciousness, and will; the mind as opposed to the body...In the Bible, the creative, animating power or divine influence of God (Joel 2:28).[42]

Many parents who have experienced a SIDS death report a "spiritual" forewarning, typically described as a "voice of power," a visual perception, or the sensation of a strong, invisible presence. This experience occurs when the individual is awake and fully conscious of his or her surroundings. The event often has such a profound effect on the parent that it is permanently etched in memory as the time at which they knew, without a doubt, that their child would die.

Feelings of a strong presence were also reported by Julie and her husband. Several days prior to her baby Isaac's death, Julie was looking at her son in his cradle and had a spiritual feeling that someone, or something was in the room with them looking on. A few days prior, her husband had been lying in bed, awake, when he suddenly visualized their son lying in his cradle not breathing. The night of the death they both had a vague feeling that someone was in the house with them. They felt something had happened, but they did not know what. They were expecting Julie's parents to arrive around midnight, but inexplicably she told her parents, "We will leave a key for you in case we are not home." The infant died later that evening and they were at the hospital when her parents arrived.

• • • • •

In addition to strong feelings of loss, Nancy heard a very distinct voice, informing her of her son Nicholas' impending death.

> I was pregnant and one morning I felt like this baby was going to die of SIDS. My husband had been state treasurer of the March of Dimes for eight years so I told him that I had this concern. He minimized it and quoted me the per capita figures of babies who die. We didn't know anyone who had a baby die of SIDS. I began reading the death notices. We interviewed some pediatricians, and they said that I shouldn't worry, that I was healthy, I exercised, I didn't use drugs or alcohol and, besides, you can't do anything about it (SIDS) anyway. I was really concerned that the Lord was preparing me for the death of my baby. Nicholas was born nine pounds, fourteen ounces and was twenty-four inches long. He was a wonderful baby. When he was three and a half months old I was standing in my family room holding him, swaying, and I heard a voice say to me, "Your time is limited/near, close." I went back to work two weeks later. I told a friend that I was afraid Nicholas was going to die, and I said that I couldn't live with it. Two months later he had a cold. We took him to the doctor. Seven hours later he died in his sleep. The diagnosis was Sudden Infant Death Syndrome.

· · · · ·

Cindy wrote

> I remember that while I was pregnant I had thought of how I knew that my baby would not grow up. I did not know how or when, only that he would not grow up.
>
> When my son was seven weeks old, my sister-in-law and cousin were visiting, and I was going to take a nap. I said, "I can't leave him, I don't want him to die." They thought I was crazy. While the EMTs were at my house working on Zack I remember talking to God saying, "So this is what you meant. I know you warned me but please reconsider."

She mentioned that she had told family and friends, and in the past had had several other experiences, always while she was awake, that also came true.

Cindy feels that sensing something was going to happen has helped her. She feels that she has become more spiritual and that it taught her more about life and love.

> I think that I am directed to help others, especially in bereavement and the grieving process. I have learned not to dwell on death but to celebrate life. The experience of my son's death has made me a very strong person and I try to tell my story as much as possible. You never know who may be listening.

· · · · ·

Linda described an unknown voice forewarning of her baby's death. She initially felt that something was wrong when Mary was five weeks of age. Linda took her baby to the doctor fourteen times in a ten week period, telling her physician that she felt that the child might die. Two weeks prior to the baby's death, Linda heard a "voice of power" state: "Hold her you won't have her for long." She told her husband, who comforted her and told her that nothing could be done if it was God's will. Following the death, Linda stated that she felt peaceful, believing that she could not have intervened to prevent the death. She stated that the voice was very powerful and strong, and that this event was completely out of her control.

Tina's three-month-old son died of SIDS following two distinct experiences. One week prior to her baby's death, Tina had a strong feeling, while awake, that someone was going to die. Later, when the feeling of death returned, it was associated with the sound of an infant's cry. So intense were these feelings of death that Tina recorded the events in a journal in such detail that she even reported the time, 8:30 AM, when she heard the infant's cry. When her baby did die, the time of death was listed as 8:30 AM. After the baby died, Tina's four-year-old son told her that he could "see" his dead brother. He "saw a light, a twinkling of a light, then he flew up into the clouds, saw him (his brother) with a smiling man and said his brother was okay."

Linnae described feelings that were very intense, sensing that her baby's smile was his way of saying good-bye. She states,

Throughout my pregnancy, I dreamed five or six times that the baby's father would die before the baby was born. However, the night my baby died, I was sitting and looking at him in his bouncer, and he smiled at me and seemed to almost change to a bright yellow color. I started to cry and said to my brother and my friend that I had a feeling he was going to die. I did not know when, and I didn't think that it would occur that evening. But I did feel it. And four hours later, when I woke up, he was dead beside me. Also, his father did die three days later of suicide.

Although Marilyn was not certain when her feelings of death began, she was convinced that she would lose her daughter, Amanda.

I knew that my daughter was going to die and nightly prayed that God would take me with her. The knowledge grew each day, and I told my mother that she had to leave the hospital for Amanda's baptism because I could not postpone or delay the event. On a plane trip to Denver, I was certain that her death was imminent and openly cried when we landed safely. Amanda died the day after my return home. I had returned to work and found that the picture of Amanda and me, which I kept on my desk, had fallen to the floor. The glass had been broken in a single line, separating us. I asked my co-worker if she finally believed that something was going to happen to my baby. After Amanda's death, a priest told me that intuition was God's gift to prepare us and make the death manageable.

In his forward to Betty J. Eadie's book, *Embraced by the Light*, which details a near-death experience, Melvin Morse comments that "Our society has lost understanding of its own spiritual beliefs and visions."[43] So strong is the need for scientific explanation that society tends to discount inexplicable phenomena. Spiritual encounters, involving visual images or auditory experiences, certainly fall within this category. Since they cannot be verified using scientific methodology, they may be discounted as a figment of imagination, a hallucination, or dream. Ami Shinitzky, former editor-in-chief of *Equus*, supports this view, stating,

> Much available data on "non-ordinary" phenomena are ignored simply because they don't fit into the prevalent worldview of reality. That view denies spirit as an independent entity and insists that everything that is spirit or mindlike is but a biochemical process and thus strictly a phenomenon of the material world...[44]

Several parents stated that they felt "crazy" for seeing images or hearing voices. Their infants' deaths validated these encounters. One mother wrote that her son's death finally convinced her that what she was feeling was real, that she "wasn't crazy." In fact, respondents reporting spiritual encounters were, as a group, productive, middle-income parents, without a history of drug abuse or mental illness. None reported the use of mood altering drugs prior to their infant's death, and only three required anti-depressants following their loss. The high level of functioning both before and after the PDP, the brief duration of the actual visual or auditory experience, and the complete absence of symptoms of emotional dysfunction preclude a psychiatric diagnosis as a plausible explanation for the individual's experience.[45]

Are spiritual PDPs common regardless of the cause of death? A review of the literature suggests that they are. Fischhoff and Brohl, in their book entitled *Before and After My Child Died…A Collection of Parents' Experiences*, describe a young mother's vision of the Blessed Mother holding, stroking, and comforting a baby.[46] This experience was described as "true to life" and occurred immediately prior to the death of one of her premature twins. Elisabeth Kubler-Ross, in her studies of death and dying, adds further support to this phenomenon.[47] She reports that patients themselves sometimes have premonitions of impending death involving visions of deceased relatives or friends. She challenges the reader to listen to PDPs with respect and belief.

Unlike other types of PDPs, spiritual encounters were often viewed as kind and loving forewarnings from a higher power. The majority of respondents stated that the experience reinforced their belief in life after death and in a loving God. Most of the parents in this group felt that their baby's death was inevitable, far beyond their control. Consequently, feelings of guilt, which are so often present in SIDS families, were uncommon among those experiencing a spiritual pre-death premonition. In fact, spiritual encounters were often associated with a feeling of peace, aptly described by one mother:

> There are powers that are beyond us here in this world and we can only control so much in our

lives. When our time here is up, it is up. I nursed my child, am college educated, over thirty when he was born, upper middle class in income and we were nurturing parents. We didn't fit a lot of the "typical" SIDS parents or the facts that are associated with SIDS babies, other than he had a cold at the time of death...I now know that children are gifts from God, and the experience served to help me understand that I only had a short amount of time with Nicholas and that it was beyond my control that he was not to be on earth very long...I just felt it was going to happen, and I feel that the Lord was taking care of me by informing me...I am thankful we had Nicholas for the time we did, and I believe I will see him again someday after I die.

Sandy agrees. She feels so certain that her premonitions were from a loving God, through Jesus Christ, that she has provided testimony about the experience to members of her church. Her story follows:

It first happened in late April 1999. I was eight months and a few days or a week into my pregnancy. My pregnancy had been normal; all my checkups were great. My doctor said everything was progressing just fine. This particular morning, like every other normal morning, I got up around 8 AM, showered and got dressed, I had been on medical leave since April 3 so I slept a little later.

As I was walking into the kitchen, I had

an experience that I am almost incapable of describing. It was impressed on me so strongly that I started to cry, it was a very strong feeling, a sixth sense so-to-speak, a thought. I immediately picked up the phone to call my mother, to tell her what I was feeling. When she answered I was crying uncontrollably.

"Momma, I don't think God's going to let me keep this baby."

"Oh honey, don't say that!" she said.

"I can't help it Momma, I just feel that way."

She continued to try to make me feel better, saying that I was just getting scared, since childbirth was only a few weeks away. She was able to stop me from crying, although this feeling, from that moment on, never left me.

Monday, May 10, I started to have mild contractions around 11:30 PM. I was awake on and off all night. I had an appointment with my doctor at 10:00 AM, but my contractions were becoming stronger so I called in, and they told me to come in at 8 AM when they opened. I had dilated 1 1/2 centimeters. I was told to go home for a while and call back when they started to get closer. Since this was my first pregnancy, I really didn't know what to expect. Randy and I went home, got my suitcase together, made all the necessary phone calls and waited a while. I was starting to have more pain then, so we went on to the hospital. They admitted me. I really didn't realize what a long process childbirth was, but I felt "better safe, than sorry."

I had an extremely difficult time dilating, and

it wasn't until 7:40 AM on Wednesday, May 12 when our precious child, Randall Cody Griffin, was born. I have to admit, even as I was pushing Cody out of my body, I honestly felt that, when he was born, my doctor was going to say, "I'm sorry." My feelings were just so strong about his loss. When he was born alive I was so happy! I had just given birth to a wonderful baby boy, seven pounds, fourteen ounces, nineteen and a half inches long. I was grateful to know that I had been wrong, thanking God silently.

We had a lot of visitors over the next two days. I was ready to get home with my new family and get some rest. My mother came to stay with us that weekend to help us out. Of course we were all wide-eyed with every little noise Cody made. Our "hearing" had increased. The next morning, we all got up, and Randy ran to the store to pick up some coffee for us. Momma and I were standing over Cody's bassinet looking at him, admiring how beautiful he was and, once again, I experienced that awful feeling that I would not keep my child. I immediately broke into tears looking at him, this time I said crying, "Momma…God's not going to let me keep him." I can say that I have never felt a "knowing" I was more certain about in my life. I was so upset by this that I became depressed, knowing in my heart that my time with my sweet baby would be short.

I purposely tried to ignore what I realized was God's warning. I was, though, very cautious about whom was going to care for Cody when

I returned to work. I knew a nice lady who kept children and lived about a mile from us. I went to her house on two occasions, with Cody, to visit and check everything out. It was imperative that whoever kept him knew CPR. On my second visit, I learned that she did not know it. She didn't get the job for that reason and the fact that, though she was only a mile from where we lived, she was twenty-five miles from where I worked. I wanted someone closer "in case something happened" so that I would be able to get to him sooner. I returned to work, reluctantly, on July 12. I hated leaving Cody, but I had found the perfect sitter. Seven or eight friends from work referred her to me. Not only did she know CPR, but she was only two blocks away from my job, and she was a Christian who loved children and they her. It showed. During one visit to my sitter's house, before going back to work, I told her that I just "felt" like God would never let me raise this baby. She remembers me telling her that.

I can remember on different occasions, again ignoring these feelings. I told a friend whom I worked with, who had lost a child twenty years ago, that I would absolutely die if something were to happen to Cody. I distinctly remember thinking about those "premonitions" at that moment. I also can remember on two occasions, seeing Randy walk through our house, holding Cody, loving him and playing with him, knowing he had no idea. I remember feeling so sad because Randy loved Cody with all his heart, as I did, and I knew that he would never see our child grow up. I knew that it would break his heart when the time came.

I did not tell my mother of my last premonition at this particular time because I thought I really was losing my mind…or was well on my way. I did not want to worry her. Every afternoon, when I got home from work, Cody and I sat in the recliner and had our "quality time." We would do the "ride the bicycle thing" and what I called the "booden, booden, poop." This he really loved; it would always make him laugh. I would take my finger and make his bottom lip flip downward twice and then in a high pitched tone, I would tap his nose. While we were playing this game his smile suddenly turned into the most serious look, an "adult" look. Cody looked me straight in the eyes, as if to say, "Mom…I'm not going to be here much longer." At that moment I looked at him as if to say, "I know." Cody was just three months old. He could not speak. When this happened, I remember distinctly saying, "God…please don't take my baby." It frightened me to the point that I had to get up, sit him in the chair, and walk away. I walked into the kitchen, trembling and shaken, thinking, "What's wrong with me…am I losing my mind? Why am I feeling this way?" At that time, I really thought I was losing it. I didn't know how or why I would lose Cody, but I knew it would happen. And I knew it wouldn't be long. Randy got home just minutes afterward, and Cody had started to cry. I picked him up and looked into his eyes. Cody's eyes were rolled back.

About a week after that last experience, on Tuesday, August 17th, I received a call from my sitter. Something had happened to Cody. On August 18th our baby died from SIDS, Sudden Infant Death Syndrome, after being removed from the life support system he had been on since the day before. Cody took his last breath, and the doctor said he was sorry but it was over. Holding Cody in my arms, I looked up at my mother..."I told you this would happen" were my first words spoken.

Though I had received advanced warning, I felt complete devastation and overwhelming sadness. It was then that I realized that I hadn't been crazy after all. Unfortunately...I had been right. I knew.

I have since supported the SIDS Alliance of Georgia, although I will always believe that SIDS is nothing more than the will of God. I believe that all SIDS babies come here with a divine purpose, and once their mission is fulfilled, they are called back home. Babies don't just die without a reason. SIDS babies show no signs of suffering, and physicians cannot find anything medically wrong with them that would cause their death. SIDS is a medical mystery. I believe SIDS has a divine explanation. It is as if God himself reaches in, takes their soul, and leaves their bodies to die. Like it is "meant to be."

What happened to me was real. God prepared me. The experiences I had absolutely came from Jesus Christ, through the Holy Spirit. I know this without a shadow of a doubt. I know I was warned because Jesus loved me so much. He knew my heart and He knew that I would need this preparation. He knew beforehand that Cody would not stay with us. Jeremiah 1:5 supports this: "Before I formed thee in the belly I knew thee; and before thou camest forth out of the womb I sanctified thee..." The Lord knows all of our needs even before we do. I also believe, with all my heart, that anyone who has a premonition can pray about it; beg God to let you keep your baby if it is his will. I believe it has the possibility to change things. But I also believe that whatever happens, He has a reason and I need to trust Him. I did, and my story doesn't end here.

I had a vivid dream just a few months after Cody's death, in November of 1999. I could see myself in this dream, and a voice spoke to me saying, "You will have another child, it will be a girl, and God will let you keep her." When I woke up, I told my husband Randy about it. I thought it was a strange dream at the time, but was so clear and vivid. I never forgot it, but I was still engulfed in grief over losing Cody and just didn't give it much thought.

One year later, also in November, Randy went out of town on a hunting trip. I was alone and "something" told me to pray about having another child. It had been one year and three months since we had lost Cody. We were healing, but very lonely inside. I sat down and prayed to God: "Lord, if it is in your will to send us another child, then send me a sign of some kind to let me know. In Jesus name I pray, Amen." The very same night, I had another dream. In this dream, I was in the hospital and the doctors were handing me my baby. I unwrapped the blanket, saw it was a girl, and burst into laughter. At that moment, in the dream, I realized that it was God who had sent me the first dream and I knew I would not lose this child.

Randy called the next morning before I left for work, and I relayed the dream to him. He said he also felt it was a sign from God. A few days later, though, doubt crept into my mind. I could not stop thinking about the dreams, so I looked in the Bible to see if God or his Angels revealed the future in dreams. I found examples of this in several places (Matthew 1 & 2, and 1 Kings 3 for example), reinforcing my conviction that the dreams were God sent.

But the pain of Cody's death was crushing. I needed further confirmation that I would not have to experience such a loss again before I could face a future pregnancy. I prayed about it. A few days later, I had a third and final dream. I dreamt that my cousin Beth was talking with a woman I did not know. I walked up to join the conversation. The woman turned and looked at me, turned back to Beth, and said, "She's going to have a baby girl!" with excitement in her voice. Upon awakening, I could not dismiss the fact that God had given me three preparations for losing Cody, and now I had three dreams about a future child. I knew the time was right to try. I gave testimony at my church that I believed God had come to me in these dreams. I knew He would send us another baby.

On November 1, 2001, I found out I was pregnant with our second child. I knew immediately, in my heart, that this was the little girl God had promised me in my dreams. I told everyone I knew about my dreams prior to the ultrasound on January 23, 2002. I was seventeen weeks pregnant. Our little girl, Emily Faith Griffin, will be born around July 5, 2002. I know that God will let us keep her. God will keep his promise. I don't know why God blessed me the way He has. But I know one thing for certain: dreams do come true.

"I Know That I
Saw an Angel"

*Premonitions of Relatives, Friends, and
Health Care Professionals*

Several of the study questionnaire responses mentioned family members who had PDPs or strong spiritual experiences. Some of these were coincidental with the parents, others singularly experienced. Subsequently these relatives and friends were contacted and interviewed. Family members, grandparents and siblings also related their stories at various conferences.

The profound spiritual effect an infant's death has on a grandfather is revealed in the following.

> We laid Makayla to rest on Tuesday, December 19th. None of us who were there that day will ever forget what happened. It was a dark cloudy day, exceptionally calm and a light rain had just started to fall. There was not a break in the clouds anywhere to be seen. The family and about twelve to fifteen friends gathered at the cemetery. The minister finished his sermon and as he stepped aside a hole opened up in the clouds and a beam of light shined down on the casket and the flowers and not more than one foot in any direction away from them. This beam of light that was shining down seemed to be brighter than sunlight and had unusual warmth to it. It

seemed to me to have a yellowish orange hue. Someone behind us said, "Oh my God." And several other people gasped. It caused a chill to run up my spine. I looked up toward where the light was coming from and for a fleeting second I saw two angels hand-in-hand one on either side of the light. Tonya and David sat there for somewhere between five and seven minutes. The light did not move the whole time that they sat there. When they got up and turned to leave the clouds closed up and the light went away just as abruptly as it had appeared. Everyone looked at each other and asked if they had seen what had just happened. What I do know for sure is that I saw an angel come and get another angel that day and I shall never forget how beautiful it was. Never a day goes by that I don't think about our granddaughter and thank the Lord for letting us see that miracle.

Before taking a necessary trip to the Dominican Republic relating to her husband's citizenship, Tracie knew that her granddaughter Elena wasn't going to be alive when she came back. The night before Elena's death her grandmother knew something would happen. She stated that Elena was "very peaceful—unusually calm and not her usual self."

One of the SIDS mothers wrote "The night my son died my mother knew. I lived in Houston, and my mother spent the first two weeks with us and our baby Nick. She then returned home to Georgia. The night he died, she awoke unable to catch her breath. I never told her about my dream before he died."

Pearl recalled feelings about her granddaughter, Hannah:

> This was my son and daughter-in-law's child, and from the moment of conception I felt something was wrong. Being a mother-in-law I hated to say much. My daughter-in-law is intelligent and a good mother, so I tried to find something that would be concrete evidence of why I felt that way.

Exactly twenty-four hours before the death, Pearl saw that Hannah's hands were both in tight fists that could not be opened easily. She thought this would be something she could talk to the doctor about.

> However, I never had the opportunity until after the death to tell her. I have since found this is normal behavior...I still feel very much that I could have prevented the death somehow. One month after the child died of SIDS, I had a similar experience predicting the coming death of the same daughter-in-law's father. He died in a snowmobile accident one week to the minute after the premonition.

Another grandmother felt that her grandson Garret was a very special child and that his time on earth changed her life for the better. Sandra writes,

When my grandson was born in 1990 my daughter lived with us, and I felt that he didn't breathe right. I shared this with my daughter, and she told her doctor. He said the baby was fine. But I kept sensing that something was wrong and went to the doctor's office by myself with Garrett. I was told that I was too involved in their lives. I had a lot of guilt because I let the doctor make me believe that I didn't know what I was talking about.

Cathy did not "sense" that her daughter would die but remembered an experience that occurred when she was drying her hair and getting ready for work. She felt that her infant, as a different older person, was watching her. Cathy knelt down to her and said, "Katie, who are you?" more in awe than fear. However, Cathy's mother who had come for a visit did not want to leave because of a nagging sense of unease that she experienced. Her grandchild died a week later.

In Cathy's words,

It actually helped me. From the experience of my daughter's death I felt I had been given the rare gift of catching a glimpse of another plane— that there was much more to existence than life as we know it. I felt God almost allowed us to glimpse this as chosen parents. I now believe, more than ever, that life as we know it is just one small short step on an expanded journey. We saw a little of this and will only fully understand it when we pass into the next plane or phase or whatever it is. I have talked with others who have had similar experiences (these people understand—don't think I am totally crazy). It has taught me to be thankful for every day that I have with my new daughter, but to be less afraid of death.

Susan was always fearful for her daughter Karen although she had experienced no fears with her older four-year-old daughter. She felt "driven though hateful" about her need to take a CPR course. The days around Karen's birth also found the family involved with her terminally ill grandfather, Gordon. The night before Karen died, she appeared to her grandfather, telling him that she would die first. A week after Karen's death he, tearfully and guiltily, confessed that he had known that she would die and had done nothing about it.

"I mentioned it to many including my daughter. It was actually a family fear. I had even gone so far as to pre-plan a funeral." These were Gordon's words about the premonition that his grandchild would die. "This baby's life and death have changed me from within" he concludes.

PRE DEATH
PREMONITIONS:
A UNIVERSAL
PHENOMENON

The premonition study was presented at an international SIDS conference held in Norway in the early 1990s. Attendance at the session was tremendous and parental contributions made it clear that premonitions of the death of a child are universal. A selection of touching stories from around the world were reported as follows:

The alarm clock noisily announced the beginning of a new day in the small village just outside Munich. It was winter in Germany and the snow covered the countryside like fluffy white cotton. Karl, a proud new father, stretched lazily in his bed as he rose from a sound sleep. Things were going well. His home, his work, and his family were the ideals he long envisioned. But the recent birth of his son, Christian, marked the high point of his life, doubling his sense of purpose. Life was good!

As he was getting dressed, Karl thought about the future, about his own dreams and aspirations, and about his son's. There would be his first steps to record on the video camera, his first birthday complete with funnel cake and presents, soccer matches, academic achievements, graduation. Wonderful visions were racing through this proud daddy's head. With all his heart, Karl wished for a long and happy life for his infant son. His love for Christian was exquisitely intense...stronger than he ever imagined possible.

Shaking himself out of these musings, he prepared to

go to work. About half way down the stairs Karl froze. His chest tightened. He struggled to catch his breath. His eyes were fixed in a glare on the wall at the bottom of the staircase. For there was his son's picture draped in a traditional black funeral cloth...a cloth reserved for death.

The flood of relief upon hearing his son's coo in the background soon gave way to anger...pure, intense anger. Why would anyone do this? Was it supposed to be a joke? What kind of sick individual would invade his home and drape his beautiful son's picture with a funeral cloth? His heart pounding, Karl screamed for his wife.

Sensing her husband's sheer terror, she rushed to the staircase. She followed his gaze to the picture of their son. The same picture she had seen a hundred times before.

"How did this happen? Why is it there?" he cried.

"What are you talking about? The picture has been there for weeks!"

"The black cloth! Who put it there?"

The now frightened mother shuddered, "What black cloth? There is no black cloth."

Dazed, the father sat down on the stairs and put his head in his hands. What was happening to him? How could things have gone so very, very wrong? Standing and rushing down the stairs Karl tore at the cloth...at the traditional black funeral cloth...that simply wasn't there.

A few days later this young German father—with the "perfect life," found his son dead of Sudden Infant Death Syndrome. This time his wife also saw the now all too real black funeral cloth draped over Christian's picture.

Dnita is a Canadian mother who had a vivid dream predicting her son Kyle's death. A week before the tragedy, Dnita dreamt that she was at a funeral where a tiny casket was being lowered into a grave. The top opened and Kyle was the infant inside. When Dnita awoke a week later she had a strong feeling that something was terribly wrong. Jumping out of bed, she found her precious baby lifeless. The only casket available at the funeral parlor was identical to the one in her dream.

A Swedish mother described her experience with stillbirth and her anxiety during the latter part of the pregnancy.

> Some days during the last month I was very worried that the baby should die. But I told myself that it was normal to be worried and tried not to think about it. The midwife told me that everything was perfect: size, weight, ultrasound of the heart. The last time I visited the midwife and the doctor was on a Thursday and everything was still fine. They said that I should come back on Monday since I was two weeks past due.
>
> On Sunday morning I woke up about 6 o'clock because the baby kicked. About 7:30 I went back to sleep and had this dream:
>
> I saw a person without a face, in a white dress, coming toward me down a hill. I was holding a baby in my arms, and I introduced the baby to this person saying, "…here is your old grandmother." (My grandmother died eleven months before) I heard a voice behind me who said, "…the time is 8:50." "No!" another voice said, "…the time is 8:53." I then gave the baby to my grandmother.

When I woke up about twelve I felt that something was wrong because the baby wasn't moving. I didn't tell my husband about the dream because I didn't want to believe it. During the day I was very worried. I hoped that the baby would wake up and kick, but she didn't. In the evening I understood that something was wrong and I told my husband that the baby wasn't moving. Perhaps I tried to prevent myself from believing what had happened. When we went to the hospital, I was told that the baby was dead.

An Australian mother described her fears of impending death:

For me this was a time of great pain and emotional turmoil. But it also prepared me. I knew from the time of conception she would not stay here. This frightened me to the point that I became quite paranoid with all I did with her. I took her to the doctor for any minor thing. I had her checked out many times from zero to eight months and was told by my doctor to stop being so silly…to enjoy my baby because she was perfectly healthy. I did start to relax a bit after Samantha turned about six months old. I began to feel that what others told me was correct and I had just been over-reacting. Then, on the night of her death, I dreamed that she died. The next morning she was found exactly as I had envisioned.

> This was a very spiritual time for me. I don't
> believe I could have accepted her death the way
> I did without these feelings and premonition...

A father described a long-term fear for his child in an Australian newsletter.[48] Following the birth of his second child,

> ...I felt there was something wrong with him, I couldn't say what, it was just a feeling. Whatever this feeling was it made me feel protective of him, even more than you normally would holding a new baby....The midwife...told me he was perfect.
>
> I suppressed this anxiety I felt for him, I told myself it was just normal paranoia, but I knew it was different...When Mikey was about eight weeks old I got up to give him a bottle in the night and fell asleep with him in my arms. I don't know whether I was just dozing, or just closed my eyes, too tired to go back to bed, but I had this dream, or if I were still mostly awake, a vision, of me carrying a white coffin. I watched myself as if standing apart, all of a sudden I realized it was Michael and I came to with a start. Fear and dread just overwhelmed me and I couldn't go back to sleep...
>
> I was still checking on Mikey and on one particular night, not all that long after Mick (my father-in-law) had died, I got up to feed Mikey and fell asleep on his bed. I dreamt Mick was in our lounge room trying to wake me. I came to and when I looked down at Mikey...I saw he had

turned blue. At first I just stared in disbelief, then panic took over and I shook him just to make sure this was really happening. I thought it was too late, he was just like a rag doll. "Oh no," I cried out and lifted him up to cuddle him. Mikey took a long wheezing breath and woke up within seconds. Marion came in and found me crying, holding Mikey, who seemed a little bemused. It had shaken me up, I never wanted to feel that feeling again...I tried to explain to the doctor what had happened. The doctor then told me because of poor light I must have imagined it. That made me so angry, as if I was just another paranoid parent...I was, but I had a reason, I felt an instinct. I took him to other doctors, but received condescending sympathy.

With...me becoming totally obsessed with my instincts for Michael, I wanted to keep all night vigils. I...checked on him at night, and when the feeling got bad I'd go sleep on his bed...

On one night...I heard Mikey talking, so I got up again, tired and cranky, but when I got to his room he wasn't there. I saw the spare room door open and heard his voice from inside. When I got to the door, Mikey had his arms up as if held out to someone in the corner, someone I couldn't see. A chill ran through me and I grabbed my boy and said to the vacant corner, "Leave my boy alone!"

In the daylight of the next morning I sat having a cup of tea feeling pretty silly about the night before, when Michael came out with a picture of Marion's Dad and proudly proclaimed it was his "Nandad." It had been over a year since Marion's Dad had died, and when Marion asked him who the photo was of a week earlier he didn't know…we decided not to tell him until he was older.

…The day Michael died, he woke at 5:30 AM, not unusual for him, and he came into our room. Now it seems so dreamlike as he went around each one of us giving us cuddles and kisses, earnestly trying to tell us he loved us, almost like he was saying goodbye…By 6:15 AM he was asleep forever…aged two years, nine months and six days.

…As for my paranoia and my dreams, I can't explain, but to say that animals have instincts with their young, so do people.…In my heart, it was something special between me and Mikey, a mystery he has left us to ponder while we go on living…

Another mother from Sweden who also felt that something was going to happen to her baby stated:

I had vaguely sensed something was amiss for some weeks…The day and night before she died I guarded her, constantly afraid she was going to stop breathing. I must have fallen asleep of exhaustion late that night. But she was alive the next morning and I calmed down slightly. Then she died at about 2:30 PM that day. What I sensed was an inexplicable and almost crippling fear that she would stop breathing and die…I had dreams that started when I reached puberty and stopped when she was born. Details would vary, but the theme was always the same. I would find my baby dead in her bed…

Bettina, a mother from Sweden, described her experience:

I'm the mother of three children, and I dreamed about all my children before giving birth…I've seen exactly how they would look with one exception: my son Christian! (Christian died of SIDS at nine weeks of age). When I dreamed about Christian during my pregnancy I never actually saw him—he was always covered with something—contrary to my other two…I always had a strange feeling about Christian… that he was a precious loan, and I can't explain why I felt this way.

Like many others, Bettina described a wise "old" look in her son's eyes.

Christian did always look me very deep in the eyes. And I remember that "look" gave me the feeling of old wisdom and knowledge about life. One night when I fed him he reminded me of a verse in a poem which goes "Look at me, I am Death."

Mary, an Australian mother, relayed her dream:

> Two nights before Andrew died, I had a vivid dream that one of our twin boys had died. I woke up and immediately checked them both and actually pinned medals on their respective bassinets. The day before Andrew died I left him in the care of a nanny. As I said goodbye I felt actively attached to him—more than I'd ever felt before and everyone present heard me say how I wanted to take him with me. We were going away overnight and leaving the twins with a nanny...I have always felt very close to all my children but Andrew was different. I actually said aloud in front of my husband and the nanny that he had totally captivated my heart. These were the last words I spoke to my child. I wonder whether this total and absolute bonding allowed him to move on.

HIGH PROFILE
PREMONITIONS OF DEATH

Parents who have experienced a premonition of their child's death often feel that their credibility is challenged when they openly discuss their fears. They may be labeled "over-anxious" and their concerns arbitrarily dismissed. A review of the literature, however, shows that these parents are in good company. Many main-stream, high-profile individuals have not only experienced a premonition of death, but have made their feelings public. These individuals, by virtue of their position and historical prospective, could not be viewed as "crazy" or "strange" or simply "over-anxious." Their stories are well documented and illustrate that premonitions are experienced by individuals in all walks of life and that it is socially acceptable to take them seriously. Some of their stories follow:

It was a cool, sun drenched autumn day in November, 1963, as the motorcade snaked through the crowded streets of downtown Dallas, Texas. Suddenly shots rang out, and America would never be the same again. The nation stood paralyzed as the youngest man ever to hold the office of President of the United States was brought down by assassin's bullets. Those of us who lived through those terrifying days will forever remember that picture of the first lady, Jacqueline, in her blood stained knit pink outfit and pillbox hat, crawling out of the back of the open air limousine into the arms of secret servicemen racing to her aid while the President slumped lifeless in the seat beside her. What most people do not know is that the assassination of John Fitzgerald Kennedy was foreseen by numerous psychics, friends, and colleagues weeks and even months before this tragedy. Jean Dixon, noted seer and author of the sixties, predicted in 1956 that a democrat would be elected in 1960 and would die in office. The Reverend Billy Graham, renowned Christian evangelist and counsel to numerous presidents, also had a premonition of Kennedy's death and actually called the president's friend, Senator Smathers, to warn him about the president's trip to Dallas. The message, for reasons unknown, never got to the president.

About two months before the assassination of Robert Kennedy on June 6, 1968, Dr. Alan Vaughn, then in Germany studying synchronicity at the Freiburg Institute for Border areas of Psychology, began to develop a strong premonition that Robert Kennedy would be assassinated. He felt that the event would be part of a complex archetypal pattern which he was tuned into, involving the killings of John F. Kennedy, Martin Luther King, Jr., and Robert Kennedy. Many coincidences and dreams began to support Vaughn's theory. On April 29th and again on May 28th, Vaughn reportedly wrote letters to parapsychologists notifying them of his premonition and hoping that Kennedy would be warned. His last letter was received by Stanley Krippner at the Maimonides Hospital Medical Center on the morning of June 4, 1968. The message never reached Senator Kennedy, who died from gunshot wounds in Los Angeles after winning California's primary election for the Democratic nomination for the presidency of the United States.

The Kennedy family has continued to live under a dark veil when it comes to personal tragedy. Author Christopher Anderson, in his book titled *Jacqueline Kennedy Onassis*, claims that Jackie had a reoccurring dream in which her son, John Jr., would die in an airplane crash. He writes that in her later years, "Jackie had a recurring premonition that

John would be killed piloting his own plane. She pleaded with Maurice Templesman, her longtime companion, to do whatever it took to keep John from becoming a pilot." Yet on July 16, 1999, John F. Kennedy, Jr., his wife Carolyn Bessette Kennedy, and her sister, Lauren Bessette, died in an airplane piloted by John Jr. as it crashed into the waters off Martha's Vineyard in the dark of night. His mother's premonition became reality.

According to the revered American author and poet, Carl Sandburg in his multi-volume series on Abraham Lincoln published in 1939, the Great Emancipator foresaw his own death, not just once, but on two different occasions. Lincoln had a premonition of his demise in 1860 while still in Springfield. He informed his friend Lamon that he had a strange vision while looking in a mirror. He saw two images of himself. One face glowed with life and vitality while the other was ghostly pale. Lamon was quoted in his writings as saying,

> It had worried him not a little…the mystery had its meaning, which was clear enough to him… the life like image betokening a safe passage through his first term as President; the ghostly one, that death would overtake him before the close of the second…With that firm conviction, which no philosophy could shake, Mr. Lincoln moved on through a maze of mighty events, calmly awaiting the inevitable hour.[49]

The second premonition took place in 1865 when Lincoln

was in the White House. Shortly before he was assassinated, the president is quoted by Sandburg as saying,

> About ten days ago, I retired very late. I had been up waiting for important dispatches from the front. I could not have been long in bed when I fell into a slumber, for I was weary, I soon began to dream. There seemed to be a death-like stillness about me. Then I heard subdued sobs, as if a number of people were weeping. I thought I left my bed and wandered downstairs. There the silence was broken by the same pitiful sobbing, but the mourners were invisible. In went from room to room; no living person was in sight, but the same mournful sounds of distress met me as I passed along. It was light in all the rooms; every object was familiar to me; but where were all the people who were grieving as if their hearts would break? I was puzzled and alarmed. What could be the meaning of all this? Determined to find the cause of a state of things so mysterious and so shocking, I kept on until I arrived at the East Room, which I entered. There I met with a sickening surprise. Before me was a catafalque, on which rested a corpse wrapped in funeral vestments. Around it were stationed soldiers who were acting as guards; and there was a throng of people, some gazing mournfully upon the corpse, whose face was covered, others weeping pitifully. "Who is dead in the White House?" I demanded of one of the soldiers. "The President" was the answer. "He was killed by an assassin!" Then came a loud

burst of grief from the crowd, which awoke me from my dream. I slept no more that night; and though it was only a dream, I have been strangely annoyed by it ever since.[50]

On September 6, 1901, President William McKinley was shot by an assailant while visiting the Temple of Music at the Pan-American Exposition in Buffalo, New York. Just days earlier he was quoted as saying, "I have a premonition that something serious is going to happen to me in connection with the Pan-American Exposition." Eight agonizing days later, on September 14, 1901, the President died from his gunshot wound.

These are the words of Mrs. Warren G. Harding, wife of the twenty-ninth President of the United States just two days before his nomination for president in Chicago in June of 1920: "I am content to bask in my husband's limelight, but I cannot see why any one should want to be President in the next four years. I can see but one word written over the head of my husband if he is elected, and that word is 'Tragedy.'"

"As a matter of fact, I would rather have him Senator than President. Being Senator and being a Senator's wife is really a wonderful life. Of course, now that he is in the race and wants to win I must want him to, but down in my heart I am sorry."

As predicted by his wife, Warren G. Harding died of a heart attack in San Francisco in August, 1923, in his second year in office.

Colonel Edward E. Cross was thirty-one years old at the battle of Gettysburg. He was well educated, well traveled, and had served as a reporter and ultimately an editor prior to becoming a military officer. He became known as one of the toughest officers in the Civil War.

Colonel Cross was troubled as he arrived on the battlefield on the morning of July 2nd. He had a premonition of death, and in his pocket was not the red silk bandana he usually wore, but a black one. He had a lieutenant tie it around his head as the sounds of battle drifted closer from Sickles' front...About 5:00 PM, as orderlies came dashing along the lines and the division prepared to move south to answer a call for help...Hancock himself rode up in front of Cross. "Colonel Cross, this day will bring you a star," he shouted. Cross shook his head and replied calmly, "No, General, this is my last battle." He then vaulted into the saddle to lead his men...A few minutes later, Cross' was the first brigade in the division to be deployed, formed up hurriedly in the northeast corner of the Wheatfield...He then strode over to his leftmost regiment...As he reached the Fifth...before he could give the order to charge, he suddenly fell, mortally wounded by a bullet in the stomach. Cross was taken to a field hospital where he died the next day....[51]

Samuel Clemens, better known as Mark Twain, had a dream involving his brother Henry's death. He saw his body lying in a casket which was positioned on two chairs. A bouquet of white roses, with one solitary red rose, was lying on the middle of the casket. Henry was wearing one of Samuel's suits. The dream was so vivid that Samuel woke with a start, believing the nightmare to be real. Ten days later Sam received word that the boilers on the riverboat that Henry was on had blown up, killing or injuring one hundred and fifty people. Sam hurried to his brother's side the evening before he died. The next morning he found Henry's body, lying in a casket placed across two chairs. A nurse brought a bouquet of white roses, save for one solitary red rose, to be placed on the casket. Henry was wearing a suit he had borrowed from Sam—without permission.[52]

On what would have been John Lennon's sixtieth birthday, Yoko Ono, his widow, released a song which she had kept private for twenty years. This song appears to relate a premonition of his death by the "angel of destruction." Yoko continued, "They say that people start to think of God near death. It's possible that was the case here…"[53] John was said to have composed this shortly before he was shot dead outside of his New York apartment in 1980. The following lines are included:

> Well I tried hard to stay alive,
> But the angel of destruction
> Keeps on hounding me, all around.
> But I know in my heart that we
> Really never parted, oh no.[54]

The world renowned author, Harriet Beecher Stowe, described her mother, Roxana Beecher's death, in the character of Eva St. Clare in *Uncle Tom's Cabin*. Roxana experienced a premonition of her coming death after giving birth to her ninth baby. She shared her feelings with her husband: "I do not think that I will be with you long. I have had a vision of heaven and its blessedness."[55] She relayed her joy and peace in Christ and her willingness to leave her family behind. A short time later Roxana developed rapidly progressive symptoms of tuberculosis, to which she succumbed. In 1997 Edward Williams was walking in the English hills when he experienced a vivid premonition that Princess Diana would be killed. He reported this to an officer of the Mountain Ash police station in Wales, describing the premonition in detail. Shortly thereafter, the premonition proved accurate.

In June 2001, Valerie Clarke, a psychic from the United Kingdom, appeared on BBC's "Kilroy Show." The interview was recorded and televised. She relayed a frightening premonition of disaster:

> I had this dream a while ago and I though it was a bombing at the World Trade Center. In my dream I was at the World Trade Center wandering the streets—I was in some sort of barricade when the building blew up. At the same time this plane went down behind it. In my dream I was not sure if the plane had gone into the building.

This nightmare proved true on September 11, 2001, when the world watched in disbelief as planes plowed into the World Trade Center towers, shattering life as Americans knew it.

Any discussion of "high profile" prophecies would be incomplete without including a section on Jesus Christ, whose life and death were predicted thousands of years prior to their occurrence. In Genesis 3:15, Moses recorded words of promise from a loving God in response to the fall of mankind: "I will put enmity between thee and the woman, between thy seed and her seed. He shall bruise thy head and thou shalt bruise his heel." Through Moses, God was promising that he would one day send a Messiah to earth who would redeem his creation. That redeemer would come from the seed of a woman and would crush the head of the serpent (devil), destroying it forever. In that encounter, Satan would bruise the heel of God's anointed.

Further prophesy of this Messiah is recorded in the book of Isaiah. "Surely he has born our grief...and he was numbered with the transgressors and he bore the sin of many and made intercession for the transgressors" (Isaiah 53:4–12).

Christians have, since their inception, believed that Jesus of Nazareth, also called Jesus Christ, fulfilled the prophecies of the Old Testament prophets and that his death was predicted for centuries. They point to the fact that Jesus was born in the city of Bethlehem as predicted by the prophet Micah (Micah 5:2): "The Messiah will come from Bethlehem..." The prophet Isaiah accurately predicted the virgin birth: "Behold, a virgin shall be with child, and shall bring forth a son, and they shall call his name Emmanuel, which being interpreted is 'God with us'" (Isaiah 7:14). The New Testament authors, Matthew and Luke, provide historical documentation that Jesus was born of a virgin.

Serving as historians documenting the birth, life, and death of Jesus Christ, Matthew, Mark, Luke, and John recorded events with detail and accuracy which had been foretold centuries earlier. Zechariah 9:9 predicts that Jesus will enter Jerusalem as a "King" riding on an ass. This was documented in Matthew 21:5. Zechariah further predicts that Jesus will be sold out for thirty pieces of silver, a prophecy which was later fulfilled (Matthew 26:15; Luke: 22:5). In fact, Jesus repeatedly predicted his own death, his betrayal, and his resurrection. The Bible is rich with examples of predictions, based upon dreams, visions, and spiritual encounters, which were later proven accurate. As the most widely read book ever composed, the Bible validates the importance and existence of these seemingly inexplicable phenomena.

As the above examples clearly illustrate, premonitions of death affect individuals from all walks of life: from presidents, to military officers, to singers, to authors, to ordinary citizens. The fact that credible, prominent individuals were able to acknowledge these feelings and share them publicly should add credibility to what appears to be a common phenomenon. Merren Parker, in *A Time to Grieve—Learning to Live with Sadness and Loss* (2000), addresses this issue:

> ...I have been surprised at the large numbers of people who have said that, looking back, they now realize that they knew something was going to happen. A premonition of death seems to be no less common than premonitions of other kinds of disaster. Many of these people were sure also that the person who died knew. Several healthy young people have said goodbye to their parents in a very final way before embarking on journeys from which they would never return. Usually undemonstrative people have become affectionate and said things that their parents found uncharacteristic. This has been reported by parents of even quite young children, and not only in the area of sudden

death. Several youngsters who later developed cancer have been reported as showing a sudden very strong interest in the disease they were later to die of. Of course it is dangerous to generalize about premonitions of death, and memory is not always reliable, but it does seem that some survivors of death, both sudden and protracted, do have the opportunity to at least say good-byes of a kind…

Acting on a Premonition: Can Outcome Be Modified?

The impetus for the SIDS premonition study came from a desire to discover if premonitions were common and, if so, were they helpful to grief resolution. Some respondents expressed that the premonition allowed for preparatory grief, facilitating healing when they ultimately faced the tragic death of their infants. Others questioned whether or not they could have done something to prevent their babies' deaths based upon their premonitions. A definitive answer to that question was beyond the scope of our study. However, a closer look at the outcome of the Southwest SIDS Research Institute's patient population, coupled with a literature review on premonitions in general, provides some insight into this question.

Since its inception in 1984, the Institute has followed thousands of babies considered to be at high risk for sudden death. This population includes infants with histories of unresolved apnea of prematurity, apparent life threatening events, apnea of infancy, and siblings who had died of Sudden Infant Death Syndrome. When infants are admitted to the program, parents are asked to complete questionnaires concerning their pregnancy history and their baby's prenatal, delivery, neonatal, and postnatal periods.

When the premonition study was undertaken, questions were added to the standard patient questionnaire asking whether or not the parents "sensed" something was going to happen to their babies and whether or not they had "observed" strange or irregular breathing patterns in their infants. At the time of the initial evaluation, prior to documentation of any cardiac or respiratory abnormalities, 331 parents reported that they "sensed" something was going to happen to their infants. This represents approximately 3% of the total patient population. Although the majority of these infants did have documented cardiorespiratory abnormalities, none of them died. 238 of these 331 parents stated that they had witnessed an unusual breathing pattern in their babies, which certainly could have contributed to their bad feelings. The remaining 93 parents did not report anything unusual or abnormal about their babies' breathing. They experienced an uneasy feeling, without definite physical basis, that something was very wrong with their babies.

One such mother of a several month old infant was following her normal routine of folding the weekly laundry when an overwhelming sense of foreboding came over her. Leaving her laundry scattered on the living room furniture, she picked up her sleeping baby and held her. Unable to sleep or continue her work, she watched the baby continuously. At three in the morning the infant stopped breathing and turned blue. She immediately stimulated the infant and called 911. The infant was resuscitated, transported to Brazosport Memorial Hospital, and diagnosed with severe cardiorespiratory abnormalities. Monitoring and medications were prescribed. The patient responded well and is currently healthy and strong. Would the baby have died without immediate intervention? Did the premonition save the infant's life? Answers to these questions may never be known. But to the mother involved, it clearly made a difference. Another mother described a very vivid dream in which the curtains in her baby daughter's room were on fire, with flames choking and suffocating the infant. Waking in a panic, she rushed to her infant who was found to be limp and lifeless. Immediate intervention was effective. Hospitalization revealed no underlying infection or physical abnormalities. The patient was followed by the Institute because of the life-threatening episode. She had no further serious event.

Knowing that we were interested in SIDS, a young cashier at Wal-Mart recently shared her story while loading groceries:

> My mother and father have always told me how very special I was. You see, I almost died as a baby. Mom says she was folding clothes when she had a terrible premonition that I was going to die. She threw down the clothes and ran to my crib. I was apparently totally still and wasn't breathing! My father worked for the fire department and knew CPR. It was unusual for him to be home during the day, especially with the emergency vehicle. But he was, and he had needed supplies right there. They tried to resuscitate me but I still didn't have a heart beat, nor was I breathing on my own, when I arrived at the local hospital. But my Dad wouldn't let the doctors give up. Finally, I apparently responded to the drugs. They never found a reason. But no one thinks I would have survived if my mom hadn't had that "feeling" that I was going to die and acted immediately. And I often wondered why my dad just "happened" to be home with resuscitation equipment…

Another mother stated that she was totally overwhelmed with fear one day when her two-week-old daughter was napping. She believes this warning, or mother's instinct, came from God. Running into the nursery, she found the baby blue, not breathing, and unconscious. After stimulating her, the infant started breathing. Transported to the hospital, the baby was found to have a temperature of 94 degrees, confirming the severity of the episode. Studies documented significant apnea, appropriate treatment was initiated, and the infant recovered. The mother continued: "If I hadn't had that premonition, she'd probably have died…I did everything right, but almost lost her anyway…"

In addition to medical interventions, many parents discussed spiritual interventions in an effort to change their infant's outcome. When faced with the care of a high risk baby, some of the parents stated that they prayed for the infant's recovery. As reported in the May 2001 issue of the *Reader's Digest* (pp. 109–115), medical evidence suggests that faith can heal. According to Martin Jones, a psychiatrist at Howard University College of Medicine, a complete understanding of

> …spirituality's positive effect on health isn't so important. We don't understand the mechanism of many drugs. We know, from observing cause and effect that they work…Likewise, we can see the effects of a person's spiritual consciousness on his outcome, so why not use that…? It's a very powerful force.

When confronted with a chilling premonition of the death of a child, the parent's natural inclination is to take immediate, evasive action to prevent the tragedy from occurring. Depending upon the circumstances of the premonition, the affected individual might become hypervigilant, avoid leaving the child in daycare, or take the infant to his or her physician, hoping for a treatable diagnosis. What evidence do we have that any of these measures can make a difference? Historical data suggests that premonitions may, in fact, allow some individuals to avert disaster.

During World War I, for example, a German torpedo struck and sank the British liner, the Lusitania. Over 1000 people were killed. One passenger, Edward Bowen of Boston, was notably missing from the passenger list. Although he had reserved a cabin on the vessel, he reportedly became anxious and concerned the day before departure. "A feeling grew upon me that something was going to happen to the Lusitania. I talked it over with Mrs. Bowen and we decided to cancel our passage—although I had an important business engagement in London."[56] In a similar situation, a couple, Mr. and Mrs. Adelman, was booked on the Titanic. Mrs. Adelman had a sudden premonition of impending disaster on the Titanic, pleading with her husband to cancel their trip. He agreed and they survived. Many other individuals reportedly had premonitions about the sinking of the Titanic. One young man dreamt that a large steamship crashed into something and gradually sank. He recalled the dream as exceptionally "vivid." It seemed as though he was there, viewing the event with his own eyes and hearing the screams and cries as passengers perished. The dream reoccurred the night he boarded the Titanic. He took the dream seriously, making preparations to survive what he knew to be an impending disaster in spite of the skepticism expressed by his family. Since he had "seen" the chaos twice previously and had planned the family's escape, he was able to implement his plan immediately. His family survived.

In the late 1800s a mining explosion in Port Talbot claimed the lives of eighty-seven workers. Inexplicably, over half the normal workforce had remained home that day. The reason: an overwhelming feeling of dread and foreboding.

The D.R.E.A.M.S. Foundation (Dream Research and Experimental Approaches to the Mechanisms of Sleep), a non-profit organization, operates in conjunction with the Sacre'-Coeur Hospital's Dream and Nightmare Research Laboratory in Montreal. As one of their services, they operate a resource website about the nature of dreams, dream research, and treatment of patients with dream-related disorders. They address the issue of premonitions and warning dreams:

> That it is possible to know about future events not only courts the disbelief of skeptics, but also often scares people who have such precognitive dreams. Such experiences are actually somewhat common, so people's apprehension is rather unfortunate, because the cultivation of such dreams can really be a beneficial skill, much like a natural talent in music or writing or dance, and can truly become a helpful gift developed both for the benefit of the dreamer and for those around him or her, as shown by this dreamer's premonition:
>
> "I had a dream where my father had blood pouring out of an eye from an accident involving the machine he was working with, and I knew he had lost the eye. Upon awakening, I immediately phone my parents and asked my father what he was planning that day. He said

he was going to work in his workshop with his drill and circular saw. Hearing this, I strongly urged him and eventually got him to promise to wear safety goggles while he was working. Then I spoke to my mother, told her the dream, and convinced here to keep a close eye on Dad. That night, Dad phoned in disbelief to tell me that a piece of wood had flown off the saw right at his eye and shattered the safety glasses. He was very grateful and admitted to me that it was truly a miracle that his eye was untouched." (S.B. Montreal, Qc)[57]

The Bible also lends credibility to the concept that dreams may foretell future events and allow for preparation. Joseph correctly interpreted the Pharaoh's dream, predicting seven years of abundance followed by seven years of famine. By storing and saving grain while it was readily available, needs were met during the famine, which did occur as predicted.

The Guideposts Book *Angels, Miracles, and Messages* is a compilation of short stories written by individuals who firmly believe that God played a role in their lives by providing them with information necessary to prevent a tragedy or intervene in a potentially life-threatening disaster. The editors state: "He continues to speak to us in whispers and dreams, in shouts and intuition. In His planning, there are no coincidences, just the working out of His purposes in ways that often defy explanation."[58] In the first chapter, they describe the experience of Marilyn Beis. Heading over a bridge into Chicago, Marilyn heard a distinct inner voice crying "Man in the water! Man in the water!" Although she peered over the railing, she could see no one—dismissing the voice as a daydream. Finishing her chores in the city, Marilyn retraced her steps over the bridge.

> …like a piercing alarm jolting me to attention, I heard almost the same words, but this time unmistakably real and urgent…This time, when I looked over the railing, I saw a frightening and pathetic sight. Thirty feet below, in the river, was a man fully clothed. He was only about ten feet from the dock but he made no effort to save himself…The man slowly began to sink under water…A lone dock worker was struggling to save him, but was in trouble himself. It wasn't until I was actually lowering myself into the water, slowly and gingerly, that I realized I was the only help the dock worker would be getting.

Together, Marilyn and the dock worker were able to save the young man. She was immediately surrounded by a gathering group of reporters and photographers, asking why she had gone into the water. "God gave me the strength," she replied.

> I was not a brave, strong person, but an ordinary woman with the usual fears and hesitations. I was able to overcome my weakness and jump into the water to help, only because of God's guidance and protection. The mysterious forewarning on the bridge that had been my preparation, the sudden decision to act and the strengthening prayers that attended me in

the river—all had come from God…I silently thanked God for saving his life. Later I learned that he was only twenty-eight years old.[59]

In another Guidepost story, Edward Cushing, a Chicago firefighter, had a dream about three people trapped in a burning building. Although he pulled them out and administered CPR, he was told that two of the three had died. He cried out "No!. . They are all alive!" Waking in a panic, drenched with sweat and heart pounding, he was relieved to realize it was just a dream. The next day was Christmas Eve, and he was assigned to duty. Just before midnight, the call came in: a building was on fire and people were trapped. Edward knew what he would find. He pulled out a woman and child, both requiring CPR. Then, staring up at the blazing building he was hit with the full impact of his premonition.

Three people. There were three people in my dream. Someone else is in there! I dashed back into the house. My men would have found any additional victims on the ground floor, so I headed through the smoke toward the stairs…. Near the top, I spotted him—a boy lying on his back, unconscious.

He had no carotid pulse. His eyes were dilated. I scooped him up and blew into his mouth, giving him fast cardiac compressions…I carried him down the steps and outside. As I knelt to lay the boy next to his mother, I felt his heart turn over like a tiny motor. He was alive…

The mother and two children survived. In a later conversation with the mother, Edward told her about the dream. "That dream was a warning, a message not to give up on you and to go back in and find the boy. I didn't save you. God did." Edward Cushing summarized the experience: "I wasn't the hero. I'd been told what to do on Christmas Eve when I was awakened by the most vivid dream of my life. In a sense, like all good fire fighters, I was just following orders."[60]

Alan Vaughan, PhD, in an article entitled "Premonitions and How to Deal with Them" states that premonitions of death, disaster, and danger are the most common kind of psychic experience. He questions whether or not acting on premonitions can save lives, then documents case histories in which such actions apparently did prevent tragedy. Two especially convincing examples follow:

> On February 9, 1942, Mr. and Mrs. C stopped for the night at a small hotel in Selma, North Carolina. Early the next morning Mrs. C dreamed that the hotel was reduced to burning ruins by an explosion. The dream woke her and she was unable to go back to sleep. Waking her husband she insisted that they leave at once. Mr. C, heavy with sleep, protested loudly that they had not planned to leave for hours. But his wife was determined and they departed at once.
>
> A day later Mrs. C called her husband's attention to a story in the morning paper. It was an account of how a truck loaded with dynamite had crashed into a small hotel and the result of the explosion had destroyed the building. The hotel was the one in which they had stayed the night before. If they had stuck to their original

schedule they would still have been in the hotel
when the truck load of death arrived.[61]

Another case cited by Vaughn demonstrated how acting
on a premonition saved the lives of many elderly patients.
In February, 1981, Mrs. Frances Vernier, who ran nursing
homes in the San Jose area, had a horrifying dream that one
of the homes was burning. Elderly patients were burning
in their beds. From 2 AM until dawn Mrs. Vernier worried about the vivid dream. She then drove to the Saratoga
Place convalescent center where she discovered a fire burning around gas pipes near the furnace. The fire department
was called and the patients evacuated. According to the fire
chief, Victor Marino, "With her dream and her intuition,
Mrs. Vernier prevented a major disaster. In just a few more
minutes there would have been an explosion—and those
people would have been killed."[62]

Uri Geller, famous spoon-bending psychic, was ready
to take a train in London when his brother-in-law, Shipi
Shtrang, pleaded with him to go by car. Uri heeded the
warning. On the way to a BBC TV interview, he heard the
details of the Paddington rail disaster, the train in which he
planned to go, in which many people were killed or injured.
Mr. Geller firmly believes that his brother-in-law's premonition prevented him from injury or even death.

Dr. Bruce Goldberg, in *Custom Design Your Own Destiny*,
supports the belief that outcome can be changed. He elaborates: "We must not neglect the effect of free will on the course
of events. A certain future foreseen by an observer involves
activities that are not fixed, since the observer can alter their
behavior and avoid the presupposed catastrophe…"[63]

Can parents do anything to avoid the foreseen death of a child? The answer to that question remains unknown. If the premonition involves drowning, perhaps it is prudent to keep the child away from water. If the premonition is so detailed that it gives time and place, perhaps it is better to avoid that location at the predicted time. But what about Sudden Infant Death Syndrome, where the child dies suddenly, usually during sleep? It is not practical for a parent to remain hyper-vigilant and awake during every one of their baby's sleep periods. Nor is it proven that immediate intervention, even if the parent did happen to be observing the baby at the onset of the event, would necessarily prove successful at preventing such a death. Respiratory and heart-rate traces of babies dying while on recording devices show that slowing of the heart occurs at the beginning of the majority of these sudden deaths—an event which cannot be observed. What, then, should be the course of action for the parent dealing with a premonition of their child's death? Acknowledging their fears, sharing their concerns with others, consulting the infants' physician to rule out any treatable and identifiable problems, and ensuring a safe environment for their baby seem to be the most logical approaches. Will these measures always prevent the death? Absolutely not. Is it *possible* that a death could be prevented? As seen above, perhaps. In view of the uncertainty of the future, perhaps the most meaningful and important thing the family could do would be to cherish every precious moment they have with their infant.

Understanding Premonitions: A Closer Look at the Inner Self

Each person who participated in the original study, when personally interviewed, was asked if their story could be included in a book about premonitions and SIDS. All participants gave their permission and the majority requested that their first names and that of their infant be used.

The concluding questions of the study were "What effect, if any, has your 'sensing' that something was going to happen to your baby had on your grieving process? What do you feel the meaning of your experience is? Can others learn from your experience?" As each individual was interviewed, in person or by phone, their printed responses were probed. Over half of the respondents initially felt guilt, helplessness, and anger with their inability to prevent their baby's death. These feelings were related to a belief that they should have acted on their premonitions and been a stronger advocate for their precious infant. Fortunately, working through their grief often led to a more positive resolution.

Laurie, a medical doctor stated, "It was a positive effect even though it was a torment. It was meant to be." She felt that the premonitions prepared her, though nothing could be done. "I don't know what it means but I hope it means something beyond what we see. Others seem to find comfort in sharing my story," she concluded. Tracie felt that the experience had "no meaning." In contrast, Lori felt that "Mothers have an intrinsic bond with their children that enables them to know when something isn't right. You should trust your instincts." Amy confirmed the same in calling the PDP "a lesson in trusting the gut instincts that you have."

Robert wrote, "Life is as fragile as a bubble." He believes one cannot take one instant of life for granted. Many replied that they felt their faith and belief in God was strengthened by the experience. Susan wrote, "God works in strange ways" and another mother stated that both her belief in God and an afterlife was strengthened. She felt better in being prepared. Another respondent wrote, "I look at all this as an attempt of my inner psyche to warn and prepare me and it has helped my grieving and acceptance. I believe in an inner sense of perception that's difficult to put into words."

Jan felt that her premonition was a God given gift to prepare her for the heartbreak and joy that life bestows. Referring to parents who also had a premonition of their child's death, Jan wrote, "Finally someone understood and affected parents could share their experiences. No! They are not crazy! This is a topic that should be studied very deeply. God bless the study."

Information was also gathered from parents who wanted to share their stories after completion of the study. As discussions took place at conference presentations, the similarity of statements and the openness and candor about PDP experiences reinforced initial findings. With the exception of one person who spoke out at a conference in Washington, DC stating that the study was the work of the devil, all conference evaluations have been favorable. Correspondents for two SIDS newsletters critiqued sessions for the 1999 national conference in Atlanta. The Orange County newsletter stated, "One of the most popular sessions conducted was *Premonitions of SIDS*. The touching stories related by many in the audience had quite an emotional effect on those in attendance." Dawn Butler, in the quarterly publication of the SIDS Foundation of Southern California, wrote

> *Premonitions of SIDS* was a discussion that really opened my eyes. I had not really given it much thought before. We met several people and we talked about it, but I never really thought that I had some insight into my Daryna's death. When I began to think about it, I realized that I did have premonitions of her death. I would kiss Daryna's chubby cheeks and think to myself, "I better get my kisses in now because she won't always be around."

Robert Sachs, one of the study participants, has published the story of his daughter's death in a book entitled *Rebirth into Pure Land*, a journey seen through the heart of his Buddhist faith. He says,

> I have learned over the years from my conversation with others who have been in the presence of death, that they witnessed omens and signs before and after the time of dying. For these persons such occurrences were miraculous and transformative. In actual fact, I believe such occurrences are normal; they happen all the time. It is just a matter of how awake one is at the time they take place. It seems that life is constantly giving us opportunities to wake up, become conscious—to see what is and is not important in the course of our lives.[64]

The following letter came to the Southwest SIDS Research Institute from Lisa L. Diamond.

I recently took part in your study of the "Impact of Premonitions of SIDS on Grieving and Healing." Two days ago, I received my copy of your findings. I wanted to take the time to write and tell you how grateful I am to have been able to read this.

So much of what I went through with my own personal experiences at the time of my son's death made me think that I was crazy—and or morbid. How else could I explain the fact that I kept having the feeling that he was going to die? Your study not only made me realize that I was not crazy, but also not alone. Furthermore, it helped to validate my feelings. There must have been something to those feelings for so many other people to experience similar feelings, and then to have the same terrible outcome. I can only hope and pray that some day, perhaps because of this study, doctors will stop chalking up all "irrational" fears to over anxious, over cautious parents, and will take the time to listen to what they are saying, and truly realize that nobody knows their child better than his/her own parents.

EPILOGUE

"The experiences that are called 'apparitions'—the whole so called 'spirit world,' death, all these Things that are so closely related to us, have through our daily defensiveness been so entirely pushed out of life that the senses with which we might have been able to grasp them have atrophied." Rainer Maria Rilke[65]

It has been over ten years since the SIDS and Premonition Study was completed. During those years the Back to Sleep Campaign, which urges parents to place their infants on their backs for sleeping, has brought about a 40% decrease in the number of SIDS deaths. However, the definitive reason for the cause of such good news is not known and science cannot yet explain it. In the recent decade, families are becoming increasingly aware of the fact that a family member often has a premonition of the SIDS event. Conferences, written information and internet communication have proven to be sources of confirmation and healing. As our study confirmed, those who were able to express and deal with the complexity of a premonition found support in the sharing of their experiences. Unfortunately, studies confirming the validity of various psychic phenomena, some now in the literature of mainstream medicine and psychology, remain unknown to many individuals experiencing a premonition. As a result, the death of their infant can be compounded with pain and anxiety. The effect of a lowered death rate from SIDS, the availability of new medical information and opportunities to deal with "the sudden and unexpected death" of their infant does not seem to have eliminated some sense of guilt in these individuals. The families who shared their stories in this book have truly demonstrated, through their compassion and search for understanding, that those experiencing premonitions are "not alone." It is our hope that this will aid in the healing process.

How very distant the time seems since we slipped that question into Southwest SIDS Research Institute's database questionnaire: "Have you ever sensed that anything would happen to your baby?" Easily remembered, however, are the first responses in the affirmative. The project built its own path. Most inspirational was the openness, the willingness, the need of those respondents to share their often long withheld stories. We held out no promises to them or ourselves as to where that path would lead. From me, the nonscientist member, Dr. Hardoin and Judy Henslee have my great admiration for their skill in crafting the study and for the risk they took. When I was dubbed the Shirley McLaine of the SIDS movement the humor seemed fitting for my role. I remember well the poster presentation of our research, which I made in Vancouver, BC in 1995 at Child Health 2000: The United Nations World Congress. Medical doctors did not approach for comment or discussion, while social workers, nurses and psychologists shared their interests and questions. Shortly after, SIDS and other bereavement conferences began to overwhelm us with their interest, necessitating larger rooms for our audiences. Many interesting revelations about SIDS came our way. One theory, that SIDS parents had a hole in their knee, was an interesting study proposal. However, our team decided that crawling under tables at conferences might not be appropriate, politically or scientifically correct. Most encouraging were those we interviewed in person or by phone who confirmed that talking about their premonitions was helpful and healing to their grieving. We repeatedly heard, "You do not seem surprised or shocked with my story." And we could only reassure them it was accepted by us and joined the tapestry of other's experiences.

Since the first presentation of the premonition study at a SIDS conference, the topic, initially viewed with some skepticism, has become accepted. It is often an integral part of each program. Frequently, the Parental Perception Questionnaire, part of the initial study, is provided for conference attendees and grief counselors who request it.

It is now fifty-one years since my daughter's death. That has led me to be a privileged part of lives I could never have dreamed of. For me, the study and mystery of consciousness becomes more acute. The recent death of my husband convinces me that, although our Western science often seems to make God an unnecessary concept, science and spirituality are not incompatible. This is territory that needs to be explored. A place to begin is "the voice within."

Carrie Sheehan
November, 2006

APPENDIX

Parental Perception Questionnaire

1. Name:

2. Phone number:

3. Address:

4. Date Completing Form:

In completing an earlier questionnaire, you indicated that you "sensed" that something was going to happen to your infant. We want to learn more about this and learn how such events have affected you.

5. Please briefly describe exactly what you sensed:

6. How often did you have such a "sensation"?

   A. Once

   B. 2–5 times

   C. More than 5 times

7. Over what period of time did the "sensation(s)" take place? (Check all categories that apply.)

    A. During Pregnancy

    B. Immediately after Birth

    C. During the Newborn

    D. Period Immediately Preceding the Death

    E. Other (Explain):

8. Do you think this feeling occurred because of:

	Yes	No
Direct observation of a physical event? (Baby had choking spells, stop-breathing or blue spell?)	_____	_____
Personal knowledge of a SIDS loss?	_____	_____
Dream or Vision	_____	_____
Vague, uneasy feeling without any obvious cause?	_____	_____
Other? (Explain):	_____	_____

9. Did you have prenatal care or take prenatal classes?

     A. _____ Yes

     B. _____ No

10. If your answer to question # 9 was "Yes," was SIDS discussed?

     A. _____ Yes

     B. _____ No

11. In responding to the sensation, did you, PRIOR to the infant's death:

  A. Mention your concern to anyone?

     1. _____ Yes

     2. _____ No

  If "Yes," to whom? (physician, family member, clergy, friend, other)

  B. Keep a journal describing your concern?

     1. _____ Yes

     2. _____ No

  C. Write a letter discussing your fears?

     1. _____ Yes

     2. _____ No

D. Document your concerns in any other way?

    A. _____ Yes

    B. _____ No

If "Yes," please describe.

12. Have you had similar sensations or premonitions which have come true?

    A. _____ Yes

    B. _____ No

13. If your answer to #12 was "Yes," how many times have you had similar sensations which have come true?

    A. _____ Once

    B. _____ 2–5

    C. _____ More than 5 times

14. Have you had similar premonitions which have NOT come true?

    A. _____ Yes

    B. _____ No

15. If you answer to #14 was "Yes," how many times have you had similar sensations which have NOT come true?

    A. _____ Once

    B. _____ 2–5

    C. _____ More than 5 times

16. Were unusual fragrances or odors associated with the premonition about your baby's death?

      A. _____ Yes

      B. _____ No

If yes, please describe:

17. Please circle the best description of when the premonition took place:

      A. _____ Wide Awake

      B. _____ Daydreaming

      C. _____ Drowsy–Half asleep or half awake

      D. _____ Asleep

18. Did you visit your physician or hospital emergency room because of the sensation or premonition?

      A. _____ Yes

      B. _____ No

19. If you answer to #18 was "Yes," how many times, and how many days prior to your baby's death did you visit the hospital or physician?

20. Have you had any vision or "sensation" about your baby since the death? If so, please describe the event(s) and how you were affected:

21. Do you wear a watch?

> A. _____ Yes
>
> B. _____ No

> If yes: Have you had difficulty getting it to run properly?

> A. _____ Yes
>
> B. _____ No

> If no: Why not?

Now we would like to learn about your medical and social history:

22. Age _____

23. Number of living children: _____

24. How long since your SIDS loss: _____

25. Do you work outside the home?

> A. _____ Yes
>
> B. _____ No

> If so, for how many years? _____

26. Hospitalizations: (Please note reason and date)

27. Please list all medications you have taken for longer than two (2) weeks (why and when):

   Have you had:

28. Seizures?

>   A. _____ Yes
>   B. _____ No

29. Blackout spells?

>   A. _____ Yes
>   B. _____ No

30. Rage attacks for no reason?

>   A. _____ Yes
>   B. _____ No

31. Head injury with loss of consciousness?

>   A. _____ Yes
>   B. _____ No

32. Out-of-body experience?

>   A. _____ Yes
>   B. _____ No

33. Have you had a "Near Death Experience"?

      A. _____ Yes

      B. _____ No

If yes, briefly describe:

34. What effect, if any, has your "sensing" that something was going to happen to your baby had on your grieving process?

35. What do you feel the meaning of your experience is?

36. Can others learn from your experience?

Please return the completed form to:

Southwest Sids Research Institute
C/O Brazosport Regional Health System
100 Medical Drive
Lake Jackson, Texas 77566

For assistance in completing this form, call:
1–800–245-SIDS

About the Authors...

Richard A. Hardoin, MD, FAAP

Dr. Hardoin has practiced pediatrics in Lake Jackson, Texas, since 1978. He is a graduate of Wayne State University in Detroit, Michigan, where he earned a Bachelor of Science degree in biology in 1971. In 1975 he graduated with honors from Wayne State School of Medicine. Dr. Hardoin completed his pediatric residency training in Detroit, Miami, and Houston, before moving to the Texas gulf coast. In 1984 he helped found the Southwest SIDS Research Institute, in Lake Jackson, Texas, where he serves as Medical Director. Dr. Hardoin is one of the founding members of the National SIDS Alliance, formerly the National SIDS Foundation, where he served as a trustee for five years. In 1987 he received the President's Volunteer Action Award from President Reagan, and in 1989 he was asked to serve on the Federal Drug Administration Apnea Monitor Standard Task Force. Dr. Hardoin served on the board of the Houston chapter of the SIDS Alliance, a support group for parents who have lost babies to Sudden Infant Death Syndrome. He is the co-author of publications on sleep physiology in normal and high-risk populations and on the effect of premonitions of SIDS on grieving and healing. He and his wife reside in Lake Jackson. He has three children and five grandchildren. Dr. Hardoin balances his time between a busy pediatric practice, care of infants at risk for SIDS, and numerous speaking engagements. In his spare time he enjoys scuba diving, snow skiing, and golf.

Judith A. Henslee, LMSW

Judith Henslee holds a bachelor's degree from Baylor University in Waco, Texas, and a master's degree in social work from the University of Texas in Austin. She is a wife and mother of 5 children. She became interested in Sudden Infant Death Syndrome when her fifth child, and only girl, had an unexplained life-threatening episode at three weeks of age. Ms. Henslee is the co-founder and executive director of the Southwest SIDS Research Institute with offices in Lake Jackson. She is the co-author of publications on sleep physiology in normal and high-risk populations and on the effect of premonitions of SIDS on grieving and healing. She served on an NICHD committee establishing SIDS research goals and an American Thoracic Society subcommittee on infant monitoring. Mrs. Henslee has been a member of the board of directors of the National SIDS Foundation and the National SIDS Alliance. She served on the board of the National Association of Apnea Professionals and the Training and Education Team of the National SIDS and Infant Death Program Support Center. Mrs. Henslee has been a member of the National Association of SIDS Program Professionals and the National Association of Peri-natal Social Workers. She has been co-recipient of the President's Volunteer Action Award in 1987 and was named Outstanding Young Alumni at Baylor University. She has been an invited speaker at local, national, and international conferences. Mrs. Henslee resides with her family on a ranch in McDade, Texas. She enjoys raising, riding, and showing horses, and playing with her three grandchildren, Haley, Tristan, and Emily.

CARRIE SHEEHAN, BA

Carrie Sheehan holds a bachelor's degree in political science from Seattle University. She is the mother of eight children, one of whom died of Sudden Infant Death Syndrome, and eight grandchildren. Ms. Sheehan became actively involved in the field of SIDS following Molly's death. She served as a Regional Director of the National SIDS Foundation and Senior Consultant of the SIDS Alliance for thirteen years and is currently on the consulting staff of the Southwest SIDS Research Institute. Ms. Sheehan currently serves as an officer on the board of Seattle's Medic One Foundation. She has been a featured speaker, panel moderator and conference co-chair at national and international meetings addressing the problem of Sudden Infant Death Syndrome. As a founding member of SIDS Family International, she was the editor of their newsletter, was consultant and writer of the US Maternal and Child Health (MCH) SIDS brochure, and has published many articles relating to Sudden Infant Death Syndrome. In the book entitled *The SIDS Survival Guide*, she is the author of a chapter entitled "SIDS, Then and Now: A Personal and Political History" and co-author of the chapter entitled "The Effect of Premonitions on Healing and Grieving." Ms. Sheehan resides in Seattle, Washington. She enjoys, with her family being a political activist, traveling, writing, poetry, and reading.

ENDNOTES

1   Henslee, JA, Christenson, PJ, Hardoin, RA, Morse, M, Sheehan, C. *The Impact of Premonitions of SIDS on Grieving and Healing.* Pediatric Pulmonology: Dec. 1993; Vol. 16, No. 6, pp. 393.

2   Horchler, JN, Morris, RR. *Dreams and Premonitions.* The SIDS Survival Guide: 1994; pp. 238–247.

3   Horchler, JN, Morris, RR. *Dreams and Premonitions.* The SIDS Survival Guide, Second Edition (Revised): 1997; pp. 268–277.

4   Morris, M. *Parting Visions.* Harper Collins: 1997.

5   Bergman, A. B. *The Discovery of Sudden Infant Death Syndrome.* New York:Praeger Publishers;1986:5.

6   Ibid. 123.

7   Willinger et al., NICHD, 1990.

8   Bergman. 10.

9   National Center for Health Studies.

10 Lewis D. All in Good Faith. *Nursing Times.* March 18, 1983; 83: 40–43.

11 Halbreich U. Premonition of Death in Painting. *Confinia Psychiat.* 1980; 23: 74–81.

12 Willinger et al, NICHD 1990.

13 Morse ML, Perry P. *Transformed By The Light.* New York: Villard Books; 1992.

14 Kubler-Ross E. *On Children and Death.* New York, NY: McMillian Publishing; 1983.

15 Gruen A. Relationship of Sudden Infant Death and Parental Unconscious Conflicts. *Pre- and Peri-NatalPsychology Journal.* Fall 1987; 2(1): 50–56

16 Rando T. *Parental Loss of a Child.* Champaign, Illinois: Research Press; 1986.

17 Littlewood J. Aspects of Grief: *Bereavement in Adult Life.* London: Tavistock/Routledge: 1992

18 Papadatou D. Papadatou C (eds). *Children and Death.* New York: Eds. Hemisphere Publishing Corp; 1991.

19 Bourke MP. The Continuum of Pre- and Post-Bereavement. *Brit J. Med Psychol.* 1984; 57: 121–125.

20 Osterweis M, Solomon F, Green J (eds). *Bereavement, Reactions, Consequences, and Care.* Washington D.C.: National Academy Press; 1984.

21 Shackleton CH. The Psychology of Grief: A Review. *Adv Behav Ther.* 1984; 6: 153–205.

22 Houlberg L. Coming Out of the Dark. *Nursing.* Feb 1992; 43.

23 Morse ML, Castillo P, Venecia D, et al. Childhood Near Death Experiences. *AJDC.* Nov 1986; 140:1110-1114.

24 Komp DM. *A Window to Heaven.* Grand Rapids, Michigan: Zondervan Publishing; 1992.

25 Robert G, Owen J. The Near Death Experience. *British Journal of Psychiatry.* 1988; 153: 607–617.

26 Greyson B. The Near Death Experience Scale. Construction, Reliability and Validity. *J Nervous and Mental Dis.* 1983; 171: 369–375.

27 Schrater-Kunbardt M: A Review of Near Death Experiences. *Journal of Scientific Exploration.* 1993; 219–239.

28 Kroll J, Bachrach B. Visions and Psychopathology in the Middle Ages. *J Nervous and Mental Dis.* 1982; 170 (1): 41–49.

29 Bates BC, Stanley A. The Epidemiology and Differential Diagnosis of Near Death Experience. *Amer. J. Orthopsychiatry.* 1985; 55(4): 542–549.

30 Blackmore S. Out of Body Experiences in Schizophrenia. *J Nervous and Mental Dis.* 1986; 174(10): 615-619.

31 Katz SM, Agle DP, DePalma RG, et al. Delirium in Surgical Patients Under Intensive Care. *Arch Surg.* 1972;104: 310–313.

32 Lisansky J, Strassman RJ, Janowsky D, et al. Drug Induced Psychoses. In Tupin JP, Halbreich U, Pena JJ (eds). *Transient Psychosis: Diagnosis, Management and Evaluation.* New York: Brunel Mazel: 1984: 80-111.

33 Osis K. Haraldsson E. *At the Hour of Death.* New York: Avon Books; 1977.

34 Carroll JL, Loughlin GM. Sudden Infant Death Syndrome. *Pediatrics in Review.* March 1993; 83–93.

35 Mandell F, McClain M, Reece RM. Sudden and Unexpected Death: The Pediatrician's Response. *Am J Dis Child.* 1987; 141: 748–750.

36 Culbertson JL, Krous HF, Sendell DR (eds). *Sudden Infant Death Syndrome: Medical Aspects and Psychological Management.* Baltimore: John Hopkins University Press; 1988.

37 Rees WD. The Hallucinations of Widowhood. *Br Med J* 1971; 4: 37–41.

38 Grimby A. Bereavement Among Elderly People: Grief Reactions, Post Bereavement Hallucinations and Quality of Life. *Acta Psychiatr Scan*. 1993; 87: 72–80.

39 Freud S. *The Interpretation of Dreams*. Standard Edition, Vol. 4, 5. London: Hogarth Press; 1953.

40 Freud S. *Splitting of the Ego in the Process of Defense*. Standard Edition, Vol 23. London: Hogarth Press;1964: 275–278.

41 Rando. Ibid.

42 Funk & Wagnalls Standard Dictionary. *Spirit*; 2:1210.

43 Eadie, BJ. *Embraced By The Light*. New York: Bantam; 1992

44 Shinitzky, A. "In Defense of an Open Mind," *Equus*. Oct 1994, pp 6–7.

45 DSM-III-R, American Psychiatric Association, 1987, pp 110–111, 194–195, 205–211.

46 Fishhoff, J, O'Brien Brohl, N. *Before and After My Child Died…A Collection of Parents' Experiences*. Fairfield Publishing Co., Detroit, 1981, pp. 36–37.

47 Kubler-Ross, E. *Questions and Answers on Death and Dying*. Macmillan Publishing Co., Inc., New York, 1974, pp 26–27, 33–34, 36, 69, 153.

48 Fitzgerald. "In memory of Michael Fitzgerald." *Enigma. Christmas Edition* 1994, *pp* 11–13.

49 Data Sources include: "Abraham Lincoln," Volume 6, by Carl Sandburg, Charles Scribner's Sons, 1939; "Anatomy of an Assassination: The Murder of Abraham Lincoln,"

by John Cottrell, Funk & Wagnalls, 1966; "LINCOLN - An Illustrated Biography" by Philip B. Kunhardt Jr., Philip B. Kunhardt III, and Peter W. Kunhardt.

50 Data Sources include: "Abraham Lincoln," Volume 6, by Carl Sandburg, Charles Scribner's Sons, 1939; "Anatomy of an Assassination: The Murder of Abraham Lincoln," by John Cottrell, Funk & Wagnalls, 1966; "LINCOLN - An Illustrated Biography" by Philip B. Kunhardt Jr., Philip B. Kunhardt III, and Peter W. Kunhardt.

51 Tagg, Larry. *The Generals of Gettysburg: The Leaders of America's Greatest Battle.* Savas Publishing Co., Campbell, CA, 1998.

52 Twain, Mark. "My Autobiography." *North American Review* 184, April 19, 1907, chapter 16.

53 "'Spooky' Lyrics in Lennon's Last Songs." Published October 10, 2000 by www.cnn.com (contributed by Reuters.)

54 Ibid.

55 Wagenknecht, Edward. *Harriet Beecher Stowe: The Known and Unknown.* New York: Oxford U. Press, 1965.

56 Hoehling, pp.31–32

57 The DREAMS Foundation. http://www.dreams.ca/nightmares.htm

58 *Angels, Miracles, and Messages.* Thomas Nelson Publishers, 1996

59 *Angels, Miracles, and Messages.* Thomas Nelson Publishers, 1996: 3–9.

60 *Angels, Miracles, and Messages.* Thomas Nelson Publishers, 1996: 14–19

61 Vaughan, Alan PhD. "Premonitions and How to Deal with Them." *Fate*, 49, 1 1996: 40–44

62 Vaughan, Alan PhD. "Premonitions and How to Deal with Them." *Fate*, 49, 1 1996: 40–44

63 Goldberg, Dr. Bruce. *Custom Design Your Own Destiny.* American Book Publishing, 2001

64 Sachs, Robert. *Rebirth Into Pure Land.* Zinah Publishers, 1993; 65.

65 Rilke, Rainer Maria *Letters to a Young Poet.* Random House, Inc.,1984